ELEVATE YOUR LIFE

ELEVATE YOUR LIFE

THE MOST INSPIRING WAY TO TAKE YOUR LIFE TO THE NEXT LEVEL

Foreword by Dr John Demartini
Human Behaviour Specialist, Educator & Teacher From "The Secret"

Disclaimer

All the information, techniques, skills and concepts contained within this publication are of the nature of general comment only and are not in any way recommended as individual advice. The intent is to offer a variety of information to provide a wider range of choices now and in the future, recognising that we all have widely diverse circumstances and viewpoints.

Should any reader choose to make use of the information contained herein, this is their decision, and the contributors (and their companies), authors and publishers do not assume any responsibilities whatsoever under any condition or circumstances. It is recommended that the reader obtain their own independent advice.

First Edition 2016

Copyright © 2016 by Author Express

All rights reserved. No part of this publication may be reproduced, stored in a retrieval system, or transmitted in any form or by any means, electronic, mechanical, photocopying, recording or otherwise, without the prior written permission from the publisher.

National Library of Australia Cataloguing-in-Publication entry:

Creator: Harvey, Benjamin J., Author.

Other Authors:

Cao, Dianne | Jones, Rebecca | Martinson, Ria | Ng, Summer | Ntobedzi, Alice | Salmon, Elinor | Smith, Rebekah | Stapleton, Raymond |Taaffe-Cooper, Mercedas |Vass, Ilona

Title: Elevate your life / Benjamin J Harvey.

ISBN: 9781925471014 (paperback)

Subjects:
Self-actualization (Psychology)
Love.
Life skills.
Happiness.
Dewey Number: 158.1

Published by Author Express
From Inspiration to Publication in 5 Simple Steps
www.AuthorExpress.com
publish@authorexpress.com

Dedication

To fellow learners wanting to take their life to the next level. This book is dedicated to you.

Benjamin J Harvey and co-authors

Foreword by Dr John Demartini

Living an elevated life is one in which you experience new levels of inspiration, creativity, achievement and fulfilment. I know this is possible for you, because I'm living proof.

I was born with physical disabilities and in first grade was labelled as having a learning disability. I was told I would never amount to anything and never would be able to read or write. As a teenager I had a near-death experience with strychnine poisoning while living as a surf bum in Hawaii.

Childhood deprivation is often the source of adult dreams and aspirations. Often a childhood illness creates a great healer or athlete. Children who felt unloved wind up loving with all of their hearts for the rest of their lives. Those who lived in poverty go on to amass great wealth.

So although I didn't know it at the time, my learning disabilities set me free to follow my dreams. I discovered an irresistible desire to achieve what I was told I would never do, which was read, write or communicate. Yet today I travel the world for more than three-hundred days a year, doing exactly that.

Perceived voids, or what a person thinks is missing in their life, become their values, or what they want most. When you live within your true values, rather than those of others, you're living an authentic life.

When I travel, whichever continent upon which I set foot, there's a common theme among all people. Everyone wants to love and be loved, to appreciate and be appreciated and to live the life of their dreams.

No matter how you appear or what your current circumstances are, everything that happens is directed toward waking up to the potential that resides in each and every one of you. Even the terrible events always contain hidden blessings.

When you follow your inspirations and intuition, you can achieve what you're here to accomplish in life. These inklings and messages are links to the highest source of wisdom available to everyone in every moment.

I hope the real-life stories you read in this book will inspire you to take a step in the direction of your dreams.

If you would love to be the director of your own life, do what you love. I believe you already know what you'd love to do, you just haven't given yourself permission to do it.

When you do, you will *Elevate Your Life*.

Dr John F. Demartini
Human Behaviour Specialist, Educator & Teacher From "The Secret"
www.DrDemartini.com

BONUS GIFT

The Elevate YOU
7 Day Transformation

Want to take the top 7 areas of your life to the next level?

There is ONE powerful 'Elevate Process' you can use immediately to improve Your Relationships, Health, Finances, Mindset and any other area of your life.

In this transformational 7 day online course, Benjamin J Harvey guides you through the "Elevate Process" and how you can improve your life from the inside-out.

**Normally valued at $295
Get FREE and instant access here:**

www.elevate-books.com/you

Life Rewards Action. Get started today!

Contents

Life Rewards Action   1
Benjamin J Harvey

Manifest Your Dreams   23
Alice Ntobedzi

Leveraging Loyalty   41
Raymond Stapleton

Elevate Your Energy   57
Rebekah Smith

Love and Connection   75
Summer SJ Ng

Love Your Life   93
Ria Martinson

Reawakening Your Identity   113
Elinor Salmon

Dancing with the Dragons   131
Ilona Vass

Separation with Soul   149
Dianne Cao

CounterPunch   163
Mercedas Taaffe-Cooper

Goals for Grief   183
Rebecca Jones

"Giving yourself permission
to do what you love is the key to
elevating all areas of your life."

~ Benjamin J Harvey

Benjamin J Harvey

Life Rewards Action

In his pursuit to assist people in finding the answers to life's most intriguing questions, Benjamin J Harvey has studied the psychology of empowerment for over ten years. Knowing that reading books like the Elevate series empowers people to bring their dreams into reality, Benjamin has been assisting thousands of people across the globe to empower themselves and live abundantly on purpose.

In 2009 he founded Authentic Education with business partner Cham Tang, to help empower people to live abundantly on purpose. As a result, Authentic Education went on to achieve something that has never been done before in the history of personal development. They received the BRW Fast Starters Award in 2013 and then backed it up in 2015 by being named in the BRW Fast 100 as the thirty-eigth fastest-growing company in Australia.

Benjamin J Harvey

Life Rewards Action

What's your top tip for someone to elevate their life?

It's simple! Do what you love. First and foremost, people need to listen to their heart and have the courage to follow that inner voice that already knows what they're here to do.

Every day I hear about people going to jobs they hate, suffering *Mondayitis* and just getting through hump day. Often it's because they don't know there's another way to live. Sometimes it's because they spent so much time and money obtaining a degree at university, they feel they need to continue in that role for the rest of their life. Other times there's pressure to follow in the tracks of their parents and be a doctor or lawyer, and along the way they forgot to follow their own authentic dreams.

I would choose doing what you love any day of the week over how much money you earn. There are many types of currency in life, and money is only one of them. I've had so many professionals coming through my academy who've had a successful career and now want to explore what they really truly want to do, rather than what they wanted to do when they started their career twenty years ago or more.

Most people spend a third of their time at work, so therefore one of your highest priorities in life should be having happiness and fulfilment in your career. The other two thirds are occupied with sleeping and recreation time.

In this chapter I will focus on elevating your life through your work and understanding what I call your Shadow Values.

Can money buy happiness?

When it comes to happiness, money doesn't mean a thing. We recently conducted a survey of employed Australians to reflect just how unhappy they are when it comes to work and prove that no matter who you are, the rat race of a nine-to-five workday doesn't *have* to be how you live your life.

There's the age-old saying, "Money can't buy happiness." The result of the survey found that Australian's would sacrifice up to $10,000 of their annual salary to feel happier at work. Since it seems they're clearly committed to making monetary sacrifices for happiness, perhaps it's time to look for more inspiring ways to create fulfilling and meaningful careers.

We're all about encouraging people to live their love and earn a living while they do it, so no one has to feel unfulfilled in their job. We suggest that if you really can't stand the job you have, put the fears aside and start making some plans, because life rewards action.

How can someone get on track in their job or career?

We have identified *five core areas* that combine to create the ultimate career choice, one that you're guaranteed to be passionate about. We call these core areas your *Values TRACK*. The key to being truly fulfilled in your occupation is simple: just focus on projects that are in alignment with your *Values TRACK*.

Most people are so off track in life, that without changing their career it would be virtually impossible for them to ever find happiness. Knowing who you are is the first step to living a life of passion. Sadly, though, most schools only teach you how to get a secure job, not necessarily a satisfying one, so it's no wonder people don't know how to do what they love for a living.

Here are the five areas we recommend you look into in order to find the right career. You can also use the exact same method when looking at starting your own business doing what you love.

1. **Topics**

    What topics do you spend most of your time and/or money on learning about, talking about or thinking about?

    (For example: nutrition, personal development or marketing.)

2. **Results**

    What results do you find enjoyably challenging to plan and achieve?

    (For example: running a workshop, creating a business plan or renovating homes.)

3. **Actions**

    What actions do you love taking, practising or studying?

    (For example: public speaking, coaching or sales.)

4. **Confidence**

    What specific areas would people who know you say you're most confident at?

5. **Knowledge**

    Around what subjects do you believe you possess the most organised and valuable knowledge?

Once you know your top five answers, you can clearly see if the career you're currently in is on track with where your true value lies. If it isn't, then try something new.

My advice is simple: *get on track then have a crack.* Nothing is more important in life than doing what you love and sharing that with the world.

Why do you think people don't work for themselves doing what they're passionate about?

I think if we all gave ourselves permission to do what we love in life, the world would be a much different place. Most people worry too much about what others think, or they get caught up in their fears. Other times it's that they don't know to make a difference and a fortune sharing what they know with others.

From working with thousands of people, I've come to realise there's something that's common to everyone, which is that they love to teach others what they know. It doesn't matter what the subject is, if it has to do with wellness, fitness, cooking, parenting, organising a home, starting a business, registering a trademark, building a business, writing a book, doing yoga, property investing or development, starting a restaurant, meditating or running a charity, there's always someone who wants to know what you know.

This is your message and a vehicle in which you can make a difference in the world. When you find your message, there are ways to monetise what you love to do by simply ordering and organising that knowledge. That's why it's called an *organisation*.

I often finish my presentations around Australia with the following sentence, which I think sums up the point I'm making here today: "Share your light, live your love and do whatever it takes to be your own best friend."

Why do most people continue working in a job despite being unhappy?

People often say they remain in their job because they need the money, but this is just an excuse they tell themselves, so they don't have to look at the real, underlying issue. Sadly, the majority of the time the real reason is because of low self-worth and a low belief in themselves.

The fact is that people who truly value and believe in themselves make sure they only spend their time doing what they're passionate about and that challenges them in some way. There's a quote from the book *Eat, Pray, Love* that I often think about when it comes to taking control of your life: "Balance is never letting anyone love you less than you love yourself."

I think it was Dr Phil who said that people end up treating you the way you teach them to treat you, through either your actions or non-actions. The real problem is not happiness in the workplace but the way you value yourself, love yourself and believe in yourself, but that's a whole other chapter!

How do we make the most of the job we hate, until we can do what we love?

What a fantastic question! It's easier than you would think.

Here's exactly what to do:

1. Imagine you had a magic wand that allowed you to have any career or business you desired. Wave the magic wand and write down whatever idea comes to you.

2. Close your eyes and imagine being in that career/business for a few minutes.

3. Open your eyes and write out at least a hundred answers to this question: *How does the job I'm currently in prepare me for the career/business I truly desire?*

The more answers you write down, the more you will start to see how your current job helps you progress to your future vision, and the more you see the value in what you're doing, the less you'll hate it.

What if I have to stay working in my job right now?

If you're willing to put in the effort, have the right attitude and work on your abilities daily, then you instantly become the most valuable asset of any organisation. When you think of any big brand, keep in mind it can't exist without its employees.

Once people wake up to the fact that they are the rarest commodity on planet earth, and that employment opportunities can be found anywhere, then they're able to take back their power.

All you need to do is jump on the website Seek to be reminded of just how common job vacancies are. There are literally thousands of them posted up each and every day. What's not common is YOU. You're one of a kind, and I can't get another one of you anywhere else in the world.

Once you realise this, you're able to make career choices from a place of high self-worth, and in doing so guarantee your happiness.

How can someone find their purpose in life?

There's so much pressure on people these days to find their passion and their purpose, and they're waiting for that *aha* moment or light bulb to go off to know for certain that they're on their path.

I'd like to take the pressure off firstly by saying your purpose can change at different times in your life, so just knowing you can have more than one purpose often is a relief. The next is that you need to actually go out and try new things.

One of the most common questions I'm asked is, "Do I really need absolute certainty in what my purpose is before I go out there and start taking the necessary actions to live the most fulfilling life possible?"

Here's my answer. I was recently running a seminar down in Melbourne, and I had the good fortune of speaking with a lady in the audience who mentioned she'd been sitting at home for well over three years virtually immobilized by how she didn't have unquestionable certainty and unstoppable determination, with the highest level of vision and mission possible, and as a result she wasn't able to move any way.

In fact she hadn't moved because she'd been convinced by the personal development industry that you must be crystal clear on your message, and I'm going to tell you that's an absolute load of rubbish.

You don't have to be certain about what you're going to do in life!

In fact, you can be as unclear as humanly possible yet still take necessary actions that will allow you to be fulfilled. When I poll audiences, quite often I find that most people have been out on some kind of date before.

Now, in a room of about five-hundred people I always tell them to raise their hand if they've ever experienced love at first sight and are still happily married or connected with that person today. Normally there will be about three or four people who raise their hand. That tells me that love at first sight is somewhat of an anomaly. It's kind of like finding a unicorn. It's rare. For the rest us mere mortals, the fact is that when we start dating people or going out on dates or getting into romantic relationships, we didn't wait till we were head-over-heels in love beforehand.

In fact, when you went out on that first date, you had no idea what that person was going to be like. You might have a bit of an understanding or seen a photo of them or maybe a friend referred you. –The fact is, your first date *is not* really a date! It's nothing more than a deep psychological analysis of another human being, and you start to look at things like:

- how they're dressed
- how they talk
- if they make you laugh
- what sort of restaurant you're going to
- what sort of car they drive
- what sort of conversations you have

Based on that, you score them either plus or minus. For instance, if they look nicely dressed, you give them a plus. If you go outside, and there's a nice, fancy sports car in the driveway, you might give them a plus, but if they walk past that sports car and jump into a beaten-up 1960s Datsun Sedan, you give them a minus. After this little plus or minus game, at the end of your date you sit at home and work out if they had more pluses, even if it's just one more plus than minus, and decide to go on a second date.

This is the dating process at least for the first couple of weeks, and if you get more pluses each day, you continue to go on dates.

After a couple of weeks you start to feel a little bit emotional, a little bit connected. You feel something warm in your heart and realise you're starting to like this person you're dating.

As the weeks turn into months, pretty soon you'll start to realize you are, in fact, falling in love with this person you're dating, and of course you know what happens next. You'd sit them down, look them straight in the eyes and with absolute confidence say, "I love you!" They'd reply, "Excuse me, what did you just say? And you'd repeat, "I really love you!" They'd respond, "Sorry, you're going to have to speak up. I didn't hear what you said." Then you'd say, "All right, you got me. I LOVE YOU!"

I don't know if you've had an experience like that, but the fact is the first time you tell someone you love them, you're still not really sure if they're going to reciprocate and are a little bit cautious as to whether what you're is real.

So is falling in love with someone the same process as finding your purpose in life?

Sitting at home wanting to be crystal clear and absolutely certain as to your purpose in life, is as insane as refusing to date anybody until you're certain you're in love with them, fully committed to spending the rest of your life with them.

Guess what? We've all been there before. Millions of people around the world are going through this process right now:

- They're sitting on a job they don't like.
- They're doing activities that aren't fulfilling.
- They're making just enough money to barely pay the bills, so they can go back to something they don't enjoy.

The reason they're doing it is because they've been sold this lie that until you're crystal clear with absolute certainty as to what your next step would be, you can't take it.

My advice is to start dating some new ideas.

If you like coaching, then:

- read a coaching book
- attend a coaching seminar
- call up a coach and talk to them
- read some psychology books to learn a little bit about mindset

Start dating in the evenings or weekends, and if you continue to like the date then my advice is to intensify the dating. Go from dating to *sleeping over*. This is where you might get a certification in coaching.

Then, who knows? Maybe after sleeping over at the coaching house, you'll *leave your toothbrush*, which means you may be start to go part-time at your day job.

Then you *place clothes in the wardrobe*, which is basically as committed as you're going to get. Next thing you know you've basically moved into the house, and that's pretty much when you quit your day job altogether, and you're fully and completely aligned to coaching.

Start dating! Don't think you have to be in love or certain.

People always say to me: *"Ben, what's it like knowing with absolutely certainty what you're going to dedicate your life to?"*

I have to tell you that I don't even know what that means. I have no idea.

All I know is that right now, talking to you is inspiring to me. Sharing this information with you to help you feel liberated and experience freedom in your life inspires me. I will tell you that if I wake up tomorrow and this doesn't inspire me anymore, I'm not going to do it anymore.

One of the greatest lessons I ever got from one of my spiritual teachers was this:

"Just because you manifest something, doesn't mean you have to use it."

So just because you create the most successful coaching practice you could, doesn't mean that if you started to love property you'd have to keep doing coaching.

Learn to live in a state of transformation, but certainly at least start dating some ideas.

If you like the stock market, then do some paper trades. If you like gardening, go and learn some gardening course at your local horticulture centre. If you like travelling, go and do a bit of travelling. Just see what it's like to go on a few dates. Before you know it, you'll start to fall in love, you've opened up your heart to your purpose, and then you'll be on your way!

Do you have an example of someone combining their purpose with their work?

We have students doing this all of the time. Our entire company was founded so that people can prosper from their passion. We run free events throughout Australia and trainings in our academy, showing people exactly how to do it. You can find the programs, events and some of our client success stories on our website, AuthenticEducation.com.au. There's one story I love that demonstrates our philosophy.

I remember watching The Oprah Winfrey Show many years ago. I think it was the one of the last shows she ever did. She was talking about some experiences in her life and recalled one moment when she went into a beauty salon, and this lady placed her hands on her face. Oprah said she felt a shudder of love go through her whole body. She'd never felt never anything like it in a beauty salon before.

At the end of it, she stopped and said. "That was the most magnificent thing that has ever happened. Can you tell me what the heck you were doing?" The woman said, "Oprah, *my whole life I've known my calling.*" And Oprah said, "Well, I talk a lot about calling. I'm a big fan of that." The woman said, "No, Oprah. My whole life I had to overcome the shame and the guilt and the judgement of others to follow my calling." And Oprah said "What's your calling?" She said, "Since I was a little kid, the only thing I've ever loved doing is extractions."

Now, if you don't know what extractions are, it's a fancy way of saying popping pimples. Everyone thought she was crazy. When she told her friends at school, they'd say it was disgusting and gross, and she put it away in a shadow. She was embarrassed by it. She kept going to her day job, until one day she thought, *Stop this! I don't care about other people's opinions. I'm going for it. I'm going to honour my calling!*

Oprah told the woman that it was the best thing she'd ever experienced, and did the woman want to come on her show and talk about it? Now, if you don't understand how the Oprah Winfrey Show worked, then you may not know going on there might bring a *small increase* to your results.

This woman now owns one of the most successful beauty salons in America. Millions and millions of dollars are going through that business now, because she dedicated her life to her calling. She gave up judgement, shame and guilt and replaced them with what she loved the most: popping pimples. That's it!

The moral of this story is to honour your calling. Forget shame, forget guilt, forget judgement...forget fear! Just do your thing, because there's one thing you should know about the world, and that is no matter what you do on planet earth, someone's not going to like you. It's just a simple fact in the whole game.

A great way to find your value is to think about if you have three hours to spare in the afternoon, what would you spend it on? You'd be doing what you love, right?

You can also attend one of our free events throughout Australia by signing up at our website, www.authenticeducation.com.au, to see how you can live your love.

What are Shadow Values, and how do they help elevate your life?

Do you have behaviours that make you feel shameful, guilty, or even fearful? Does dwindling away hours scrolling through Facebook, or perhaps, sneaking a piece or three of chocolate late at night make you retreat in shame? These feelings have a name. They're called Shadow Values, and they're the driving force behind your behaviour, whether consciously or not.

Everything you ever do in life, every action you take, whether you realise or not, gives you fulfilment in one or many Shadow Values. I've spent over a thousand hours researching Shadow Values to determine what it is that unconsciously drives people's behaviour, and the findings are surprising.

By discovering a balance between your Shadow Values and Golden Values, which are the values you would happily tell the world about, you're truly able to bring mastery into your life. Everyone is seeking happiness on some level, but most don't know what it feels like once they arrive at that happy place.

Once people get over the shame and guilt they have around admitting the driving force behind their actions and behaviours, be that money, validation or even rebelliousness, people can take control of their lives. By taking ownership of your Shadow Values, you can leverage them to drive success, happiness and fulfilment in the most effective ways.

There are seven key Shadow Values I've listed below alphabetically, not by hierarchy. By understanding what your Shadow Values are, you can take ownership of them. Then once you own them, you own your life.

1. **Attention**

    Similar to uniqueness, status, feeling special, standing out, being different, prestige, recognition, achievement, adventure, creativity, variety, fun.

2. **Authority**

    Similar to giving orders, acting in an overbearing parent-like manner, being respected, having a sense of righteousness, having the power to do it all your way.

3. **Belonging**

    Similar to being accepted by, connected to or feeling part of a community, a friendship, a family.

4. **Control**

    Similar to being able to influence your circumstances, your territory, yourself and/or others, security, certainty, protection, safety, freedom.

5. **Rebelliousness**

    Similar to being naughty, knowing you're doing something wrong, breaking the rules, sticking it to the authority figure.

6. **Superiority**

    Similar to power, progress, expanding, success, ambition, achievement, confidence, morality, problem solving, being right, being better than yourself and/or others.

7. **Validation**

   Similar to being important, worthy and/or "good enough", deserving.

In addition to these, there are two other supplementary Shadow Values, which while not feeling orientated, were of significant importance:

1. **Money**

   Similar to being wealthy and/or having the power to do or have whatever you want, cash flow, equity, funds, cash.

2. **Sexuality**

   Similar to attraction, esteem, being able to express your sexual desires and/or preferences shamelessly, sexual intimacy, love, affection.

Once people are able to get over the shame and guilt around admitting what's at the core of their desire to do specific actions, they're able to rapidly take control of their lives. Until you're able to take ownership of your Shadow Values, they run your entire life. Once you take ownership, you can use them to drive your success, happiness and fulfilment in the most effective ways.

Using Shadow Values allows you to change any aspect of your life in a rapid and sustainable way. Everything you do in life gives you a feeling in return. Once you know exactly what feeling, or feelings, the action gives you, it can be replaced by another action that gives you a higher level fulfilment of the same feeling or feelings.

Here's an example:

Recently I met a lady in Perth who'd been smoking cigarettes for over forty years.

Life Rewards Action

- She always wanted to be an author, however she'd never been able to start writing her book.

- She had a message inside of her heart she wanted to share, but for some reason she was never able to follow through with her action of writing a book.

I spent a few minutes doing some processes with her to help her move beyond her shame, guilt and self-judgement, so she was able to finally admit the core benefit she got from smoking cigarettes.

If you ask a smoker what they get out of smoking, more often than not they will say things like this:

- Nothing. I hate it.

- I'm addicted to it.

- I don't get anything from it.

People don't do anything in life unless there's some type of perceived payoff, so once they get honest with themselves, and are void of shame and guilt, they give a completely different answer.

This lady ended up admitting that every time she lit up a cigarette, she got a feeling of rebelliousness.

I then asked her how writing a book would give her an even stronger sense of rebelliousness, and she started giving me answers.

Once she'd given around ten to fifteen solid answers, she turned to me and said, "I've just quit smoking, and I need to go home now and write my book."

This happened in front of a live audience of around three-hundred people, and it was one of the fastest transformations they'd ever seen.

Even though it does seem miraculous when people witness it for the first time, this is a fairly standard result when Shadow Values are used correctly. Not only do people change rapidly, but they never crave the original behaviour again when the process is done correctly.

What happened with this lady, and the hundreds of other people who have achieved similar results, is a simple mathematical equation. This lady was receiving a certain level of fulfilment from smoking within her Shadow Value of rebelliousness. If we give it a score, it could be said she received a six out of ten for her rebelliousness fulfilment.

After answering the question regarding writing her book, she immediately realised she could give a nine out of ten for writing her book and therefore changed the behaviour right there on the spot. To her, smoking became a *lower-level fulfilment* in her Shadow Values system, and therefore she will never want to do it again.

In fact, anything less than writing her book each and every day would be robbing her of the feeling she so dearly loves to feel, that of being rebellious.

Human beings are bonding creatures with an inbuilt desire to bond with anything that gives them feelings they love. Once they bond to an action that gives them what they want at their core, they never again think about the actions they took previously to obtain a lower level of the same feeling.

At the end of the day the mind is set up as a *values fulfilling* mechanism, so once it knows it can get a higher level of fulfilment in a certain Shadow Value, it never craves the old behaviour again, because it's simply illogical for the mind to seek out a lower level of fulfilment in life.

The good news is that no one needs to feel any shame or guilt around their Shadow Values, because everyone has them. They're literally built into your DNA as part of your survival. They help you to evolve and advance your consciousness. If everyone has them, then there really is nothing to be ashamed of.

If you take a newborn baby and look at their behaviour, you can clearly see all Shadow Values being expressed on some level. For example, as they get all of the attention, they have total control of a room, it doesn't matter what you say, they'll do their own thing, and they require plenty of validation from their parents throughout the day. And all of this from someone who can't even walk or talk yet!

When you're able to find the perfect balance between your Shadow Values and your Golden Values, you're able to truly bring mastery into your life.

Every action you take has both Shadow and Golden Values, and this is why it's impossible to give without receiving in life.

For example, someone who teaches others may get these Shadow Values:

- **Attention**

The teacher feels this from being in front of a roomful of students looking at them for the entire class.

- **Superiority**

The teacher receives this from knowing they're delivering advanced content to the students most of them don't know.

- **Control**

The teacher gets this from being able to ensure the class runs smoothly by setting all of the rules and making sure everyone follows along with the lesson.

Looking at it from the student's side, you can also see the Golden Values:

- **Attention**

The students get the ability to learn in a live environment, because the teacher had the courage to stand up in front of a roomful of people and teach them lessons.

- **Superiority**

The students are able to further their education, because the content being presented is superior and thus advances their knowledge around this subject.

- **Control**

The students are able to learn effectively, because other students aren't running amuck, making noise and reducing the effectiveness of the learning environment.

You can listen to an audio program on Shadow Values by simply going to this link: www.authenticeducation.com.au/shadow

So how do you master your Shadow Values when you're ashamed to admit what they are?

1. **Get Over It**

    Let's face it. We're all human, and we all have things we're embarrassed by. But everyone has them, they're inbuilt into the DNA, so the best way to move past that is to embrace them and understand how you can use them to better your life.

2. **Identify What They Are**

   Imagine you have the afternoon away from responsibility. What would you spend the afternoon doing? Whatever you choose is reflective of the greatest importance to your personal identity. For example, if you choose to visit with family, this may fulfil the shadow value of belonging. If you choose to study, this may fulfil the shadow value superiority. Just as Golden Values are arranged in a hierarchy of importance to you, so are your Shadow Values.

3. **Link Your Values With Your Goals**

   It's not Shadow Values themselves that make a difference, it's how you use them!

   If making money is important to you, and your Shadow Value is control, ask yourself how making more money can give you more control. Continuing from this example, do this exercise:

   a. Handwrite a list of three-hundred reasons why making money will give you even more control.

   b. Read it out loud before you go to sleep at night and again first thing in the morning for the next seven days while visualizing yourself doing whatever it is you do to make money.

   c. Walk around trying to emulate the feelings of being highly paid. Not *wanting* to be, but as if it's happening right now.

Once you've established how you can utilise your Shadow Value, you will no longer require motivation to take action, because you'll be inspired to do so by seeing what fulfilling your goal could achieve. In order to love yourself fully, you must first learn to love your shadow.

Then go about the business of living your love, and you will Elevate Your Life.

To discover more about how Ben can help you *Elevate Your Life*, simply visit www.elevate-books.com/life

Alice Ntobedzi
Manifest Your Dreams

Alice Ntobedzi is a psychologist, certified life coach and an international bestselling author with a great interest in understanding human behaviour. She's worked in a number of public mental health services in Australia and also as a mental health specialist for an employment service. She currently works in her private practice and coaching business.

Her areas of interest include emotional intelligence, neuroscience, personal growth, and human potential. In 2007 she co-published the journal article, "Emotional Intelligence, Coping and Psychological Distress: A Partial Least Squares Approach to Developing a Predictive Model" that was based on her Master of Psychology clinical thesis.

Alice Ntobedzi

Manifest Your Dreams

Could life experiences shape your values or even lead you to discover your values?

Values provide an internal reference for what you prioritise in your life. As I look back, I can see a thread connecting the story of my life. I was led to the path of studying psychology even before I was really clear about what my life purpose was. Like most people, I went to university with the aim of graduating and getting a good job. Later on, my desire for personal growth, discovering my potential and learning about success principles was ignited. I got introduced to incredible mentors, studied the Greats, synthesised my knowledge and experimented with a wide range of transformational techniques.

I also experienced life-challenging circumstances that stirred my heart to want to learn more about myself. One of them was a relationship breakup. I went through heartbreak, but the situation got me to dig deep within me. As I was coming to terms with this situation, I searched my soul. I connected with the higher source, nature's creation, realised the power and intelligence behind it and trusted my intuitive guidance.

I've since realised this situation helped catapult my vision for success. I'd become complaisant but awakened myself as a creator of my own reality. I had the power to design the life I desired, without having to look outside of myself.

The epiphany was about realising how past circumstances had given me feedback and lessons, and that I could create much better results from my new level of awareness. This shifted the way I approached different situations. I started to set goals guided by this awareness, and I envisioned what I wanted to manifest in my life. I began to see more opportunities coming through people and events and was guided to discover the tools and resources to help me achieve my goals. My desire to learn, grow, discover my purpose and live it, continued to unfold.

Pain is a vehicle for growth. It can be viewed as a gateway to consciousness evolution and awakening. The capacity to transform pain will determine the level of growth and evolution reached. At the end of the day, pain is unavoidable.

How does a person discover what truly inspires them?

There may have been times you've felt lost or stuck, didn't know your purpose, struggled with managing your emotions, felt hopeless and helpless, and even believed you were a victim of life's circumstances. This could be internal feedback letting you know you're not satisfied with your current path. William James, an American philosopher and psychologist, suggested that human beings are the only creatures on earth that can change their habits, destiny and the outer aspects of their lives by changing their inner attitudes.

Your significant life experiences and influencers have shaped the person you are, which includes your values and the choices you make. By uncovering your negative beliefs and emotions, you'll clarify your values. You may know you have frequent negative thoughts and admit your limitations to yourself and others, but not consider changing them. Negative patterns and beliefs you're aware of but don't change, or you remain unconscious of, can keep you cut off from conscious expansion. But it's possible to discover your potential, find meaning in your life and create the results you desire.

There's an exercise that can help you become consciously aware of past experiences, as well as beliefs and emotions, that likely have influenced your life and hindered your success. It involves reviewing your life experiences from birth all the way up to recent times. As Steve

Alice Ntobedzi

Jobs said, "You can't connect the dots looking forward. You can only connect them looking backwards, so you have to trust that the dots will somehow connect in your future."

Aristotle said "knowing yourself is the beginning of all wisdom". By doing this exercise, I was able to trace back some experiences I believe contributed to my fear of public speaking. They say it's the number one fear in the world. I remember when I was in preschool, and the teacher asked the class to tell a fictional story. When it was my turn to get up and speak, I had no idea what to say. I'd never told a story, so in the spur of the moment I decided to make up something. Realising my story had to be unique, I started by saying, "Once upon a time there was a horse, and it went to the mall…" Well, I immediately got stuck, as I realised a horse can't go shopping, so I didn't know where to take the next line.

In another situation when I was in grade 4, the teacher asked the class to take turns reading a paragraph from a book. When it was my turn I got up and started reading. Then I froze. That's all I remember to this day.

I also didn't do well with my junior secondary school certificate, and I wasn't accepted to the local government high schools. My parents valued education so much, they prepared for me to be sent away for three years to a private senior secondary school on the other side of the country. Prior to this time, studying hadn't been my priority, but I was able to shift my attitude, and I did well in my final year. This enabled me to attain a scholarship to study psychology in Australia, so I migrated from Botswana where I was born and raised.

Even though these incidents may seem negative, when I looked closely at them later I realised they also had a message of value for me. Before I processed the beliefs associated with them, my responses to life were misrepresented and hindered my creativity. The experiences were at an unconscious level, but once I brought them to my conscious awareness, I owned the lessons and saw the value. I then engaged the power of my mind to alter the unconscious patterns of beliefs I'd developed. This brought an alignment of my thoughts with what I consciously desired.

My re-birthed purpose to educate others and for expansion came from my early years of education from what initially seemed like setbacks. This became the driver for my aspirations. It's how I accessed my creativity and expansive vision.

I'd inadvertently developed a desire to teach, speak and inspire in my profession. It was through these experiences that I connected with my purpose. Everything worked together to bring me to this point. Before I connected the dots, I found it difficult to be inspired and often thought I had no idea what my purpose was.

To facilitate the change of my beliefs and experiences, I took a role that involved delivering training to staff and members of the community. After all, I wasn't going to continue to believe the thoughts that previously held me back. I had a choice.

> "Success is to be measured not so much by the position that one has reached in life as by the obstacles that one has overcome while trying to succeed."
> ~ Booker T. Washington

Exercise

This exercise is designed to help you understand the connections in your life experiences and events and make sense of them.

Make two columns. In the first column, write down past events from your timeline that you perceive had a significant impact in your life, as well as the negative beliefs and emotions associated with them. In the second column, write your reflections about how you believe each experience also contributed to your life and purpose to this day.

As you do this exercise, contemplate on these questions:

- What do you see as your negative or positive influences?
- What have your experiences led you to do in life?
- Where do you think your strengths lie? (This could be what your life is demonstrating at the moment and lead you to where your true power lies.)
- Have you held yourself back from success?
- What beliefs might you change?
- What emotions might you face or allow room for?
- What insights can you now take into your future?
- Can you change your current course?
- What's the bigger picture for you?

> "Life is a series of experiences, each one of which makes us bigger, even though it is hard to realize this. For the world was built to develop character, and we must learn that the setbacks and grieves which we endure, help us in our marching onward."
> ~ Henry Ford

How can people overcome the limitations caused by their unconscious mind?

The unconscious mind is the gateway to communication with your creative power. It collects sensory data throughout your lifetime and uses the stored data to guide decisions. This means the information that currently guides your life could be redundant, and as a result protect you from growing. If you wish to improve your results and outcomes, but your unconscious mind is not in line with what you desire, then you'd struggle.

Lack of alignment is the reason you'd find it difficult to get motivated and tend to procrastinate when it comes to taking action. The resistance is at an unconscious level. It's the beliefs you aren't aware of that drive you to unwanted negative results. You're also likely to miss out on opportunities because of these limitations. In order to make inroads, exploring the structure of the inner mind is necessary. Your unconscious mind follows your lead. It's receptive and absorbs information given to it. The more you persuade it by changing your beliefs, behaviours and emotional reactions, the more it will respond.

> "Until you make the unconscious conscious,
> it will control your life and you will call it fate."
> *~ Carl Jung*

How can people change their beliefs and improve their results?

The examples I shared from my school experiences formed and reinforced the belief, *I don't want to say the wrong thing.* I invite you to look into your childhood, as well as later years, for experiences that stand out for you.

Successful people have ways to deal with the mental obstacles or resistance to change, but if you don't know this, your beliefs can stop you from achieving your goals. You can learn to intentionally nourish your mind and improve the quality of your thoughts. Your brain is always adapting to your thought patterns, whether negative or positive. There's a process that combines reframing, relaxation, imagery rehearsal, and self-talk scripts that can assist you.

Here is the seven-step process:

1. Write down the belief you want to change. For example, *I don't want to say the wrong thing.* Beliefs come in clusters, so identify as many as you can think of concerning an issue you want to work on.

   Another way to pinpoint your beliefs is to observe your thoughts when you're about to take on a new challenge. Also note what you tend to avoid and why. The most common beliefs include thinking you're not good enough or smart enough, that you don't have what it takes or are undeserving and unlovable. These examples are general. In order to get the most out of this exercise, you need to be more specific. Drill down to the main issue from any aspect of your life. What's the worst-case scenario or excuse that relates to your belief? What stops you in your tracks?

   From the beliefs you've identified, pick the top three or the main one that if you changed it, would make a difference in your growth or in the area of life you wish to improve upon. These are some questions to ask yourself:

   - Is this belief a hundred percent true?
   - What's the evidence against this belief?
   - What feedback am I getting from others that contradicts the belief?

- What are the drawbacks of holding onto this belief now and in the future?

- What's an alternative, realistic and more balanced belief I can adopt?

2. The emotions that come along with these beliefs increase the resistance to change. For instance, fear, embarrassment, discomfort and distress. The mind looks at the past situation that formed the belief, and this rear-view mirror process becomes an automatic reminder. As long as in your mind you believe you'd have the same feelings, you'd take steps to avoid the situation.

   Face your triggers. Acknowledge the emotion, label it, give room for it, sit with it and don't push it away. Breathe calmly, observe it without exaggerating its importance and let it pass. Experiencing challenging emotions with self-compassion rather than being self-critical is related to emotional intelligence, confidence and self-esteem.

3. Beliefs are not facts, so try not to generalise. If something happened in the past, that doesn't mean it would happen in the future. This assumption keeps the belief in place. Be open to a different outcome. When you stop avoiding the situation, you have a higher chance of changing and mastering new skills. The older version of you is more resourced to learn new skills compared to the younger version.

4. Try to avoid filtering. Are you magnifying the negatives and minimising the positives of a situation? This can lead to distorted thinking, because you only tell yourself one side of the story. You don't want to keep playing a self-punishing story and reinforce a self-fulfilling prophecy. List all of your positive qualities, achievements and reasons why you're good enough and smart enough. To reinforce your thinking, re-read the list regularly.

5. Use imagery rehearsal. This involves spending a few minutes in a quiet place and doing visualisation. You can change the content and the outcome of the imagery, whether it's a past memory (reminder) or a future event (feared). Relax by taking a few deep breaths, and then continue to breathe easily and naturally, in through your nose, eyes closed, becoming aware of any tension or sensations in your body, and then letting the tension go with each breath out through your mouth.

   Allow yourself to focus only on your body. If your mind wanders, bring it back to the body part you're working on. Silently notice your scalp relaxing as you breathe. Then sense and relax each part of your body, all the way down to your feet. Continue breathing and repeat silently, *My whole being is completely relaxed*. Notice the pleasant physical sensations in your body, and bring a gentle smile to your face as you take in a deep breath and appreciate the moment.

   Visualise in detail an image of the outcome you would like to create, while engaging all of your senses to make the image more dynamic. As if you're in the desired creation, notice the sounds, smells, sensations, objects, and colours around you. Relive your empowering actions and feelings. For example, if you fear public speaking, see yourself in front of a roomful of people where you feel relaxed, safe and confident. You're smiling, standing up straight and talking eloquently, while feeling welcomed and supported.

   The process of visualisation saturates your mind with images, sounds and feelings, which essentially reprograms your mind with expectations of your desired outcome. You'll only be limited by your thoughts and imagination, so enrich your image.

Finally, reaffirm your new belief(s) with positive self-talk. Repeat it quietly several times. For instance, "I speak confidently, and I become more and more comfortable in front of others." It might be helpful to draw upon your responses from the previous exercises regarding your new beliefs about yourself. See yourself in your mind's eye, and replay your mind movie of the desired outcome, while feeling the associated positive feelings. You can reinforce this process by playing relaxation music in the background. It will take developing a continual habit to benefit from this process.

6. Avoidance maintains the belief and its consequences. Taking action solidifies change and replaces old behaviour patterns. What's the one thing you want in your life right now that you can go out and get? What's the first step you can take? This would be an opportunity to practice your newly found way of thinking. For example, you might take the opportunity to ask a question or make a comment at a staff meeting.

To overcome the barriers of achieving any goal, break down the complex tasks and start with the smaller steps towards the bigger goal. New neural pathways in the brain are created with new behavioural patterns, and you develop as a person. Persist, experiment, repeat, and set short, medium and long-term goals.

7. Believe in yourself, and do it. Reaffirm your new beliefs repeatedly and have fun. Write down your new belief(s) on a card, carry it with you and read it often. You consciously self-direct changes in your brain with these practices. Your mind loves to solve puzzles, and soon it will draw you to ideas and opportunities to fulfil your goal.

Alice Ntobedzi

> "A positive attitude causes a chain reaction of positive thoughts, events and outcomes. It is a catalyst, and it sparks extraordinary results."
> ~ *Wade Bogg*

A Change Management Model:

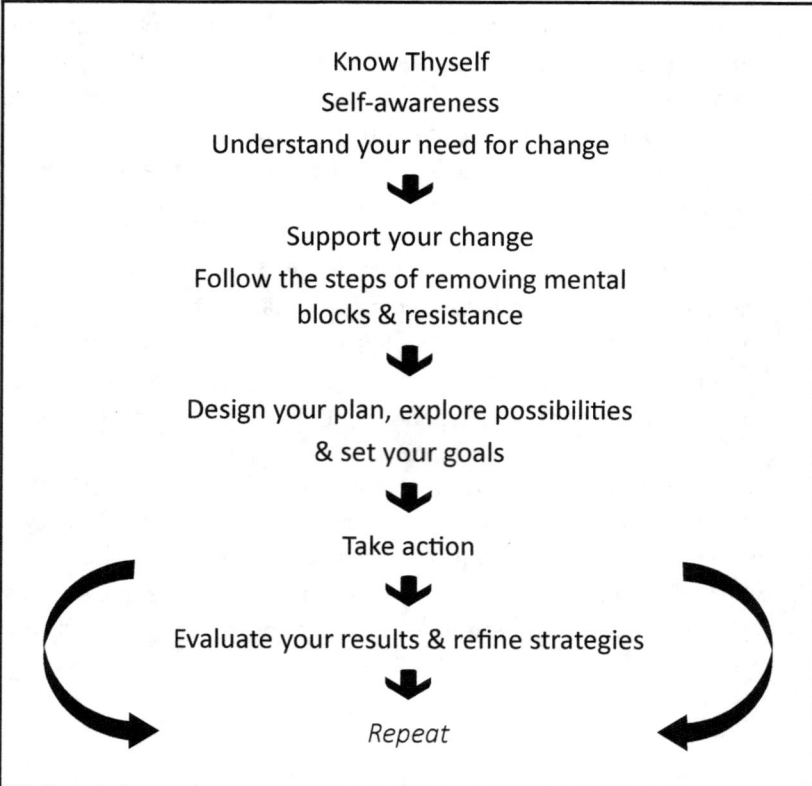

How is it possible to keep up motivation and enthusiasm?

Acknowledge where you are in your journey. Revise your goals if necessary. A question you may want to ask yourself is, *Am I following my dreams or following what's expected of me by others?* Knowing your personal values is important, because it will help you become clearer when it comes to making decisions that are right for you. There's a possibility you're conforming to the ideas of those around you, either consciously or unconsciously. When you set goals based on what's most important to you, you'll be more inspired.

What's a good method to overcome self-doubt?

Confidence is self-assuredness in your abilities, talents, and personal strengths, while self-esteem defines your self-worth. Confidence and self-worth will definitely help you overcome self-doubt and enhance motivation. Past negative life experiences may affect your confidence and self-esteem. Any experience can be a curse or a blessing, so it's up to you to determine how it's going to serve you. The meaning you give to situations determines the results. For instance, becoming a victim or a victor. By continuing to think negative thoughts, you actively maintain painful experiences and negative opinions about yourself.

> There is more in us than we know. If we can be made to see it, perhaps, for the rest of our lives, we will be unwilling to settle for less."
> ~ Kurt Hahn

Is it possible to experience a perfect version of life?

No, but you can certainly improve the results. You've probably heard the saying that there's a reason for everything, and I believe there's always a lesson to be learnt in every situation. The challenges you may experience can be viewed as an opportunity to rethink your goals, reaffirm what matters most or rediscover what makes you truly happy.

From a challenging situation, you may experience deep pain and an increased stress level, requiring you to stop, focus inwardly, face the feelings, and try to make sense of situations. These responses are normal, and you can ensure good self-care by reaching out to others for support to increase your coping ability or seek professional help if required.

At the end of the day, accepting the reality of the situation, finding the lessons or the silver lining behind it, being proactive and having a positive mindset will lead you to being in control of your destiny. Oftentimes, a situation that initially caused a setback can also be the same situation you'll have gratitude for, because of what you gained from it. Remaining stuck and feeling victimised would just lead to going around in circles and reduced creativity.

Exercise:

Practice gratitude. It puts situations into perspective and unlocks the fullness of life. Flip the coin and see what's possible in challenging situations. You can ask, "What's important for me to know?" Also, feel appreciation for what you currently have in your life.

Can anyone learn from the intelligence of the universe?

I'm in awe when I think about how the mind, body and brain function. Everything isn't random and chaotic. The mind has the potential to make the impossible happen. The organs know what to do without receiving instructions. The neural anatomy and sensory system are highly sophisticated and perfect, and they provide everything needed to connect with the world around us.

From the fertilised egg, through the process of cell division, an embryo developed into the person you are today, equipped with all you need to thrive and be a success. You can learn from nature as well. A seed germinates into a sprout, and given the right conditions, it doesn't struggle to grow. It springs out naturally and effortlessly, so once you connect with your nature as a creative being, you can express and bring out the best in yourself.

Is this possible for anyone?

When you set goals or want to change your circumstances, all sorts of situations occur that would not have otherwise. Anyone in any field can use these techniques to improve their life, such as entrepreneurs, athletes and musicians. You can make it happen by breaking through your mental barriers. Your most powerful asset is your mind, which is why every invention started with a thought. Guidance, or a reminder to clarify goals, values and visions, is needed to take the necessary steps towards what you want.

An example of when I applied the techniques to create what I wanted was when I sat in the audience at a property seminar. There were presenters with different strategies, one after another. I had gone there with a specific intention in mind, to find a way of getting started in investing. Before the end of the sessions, one presenter showed me I could do it. Although I didn't take up what was offered, I received confirmation it was possible.

Because I'd now become more aware, a few weeks later I saw an advertisement on the TV that was exactly what I was looking for. I wound up securing my first property and acquiring additional funds I used towards other expenses. Since then, I've set further goals and have used different strategies to secure more properties.

In another instance, a lady approached me while I was having lunch with friends and told me she'd once spotted me driving off and chased me in her car but never caught up. She wished to recruit me for a modelling event. This became my modelling debut on my thirtieth birthday. The designer of the dress I wore won the prize for the best design in the evening wear category, and my photo appeared in the local newspaper. Because I exuded more confidence, other people could pick up on it.

I also would like to share that prior to getting the opportunity to write this chapter, I had set out an intention to write an international bestseller. I followed the exercises I've described and stayed open to ideas that could help me with my goal. I now realise my goal was fast-tracked, and it was manifested as being a contributor to this series. I'm grateful and look forward to continuing to write.

> "Whatever you can do, or dream you can do, begin it. Boldness has genius, power, and magic in it. Begin it now!"
> ~ *Johann Wolfgang von Goethe*

What methods are helpful to create a successful result?

Everything takes practice. You can't give up on yourself. Habits can be changed. Once you become aware of your negative thinking, you have an opportunity to change your thoughts. Sometimes due to the habit of negative thinking, you can fall into unhelpful patterns, and it becomes your default position. But if you guide your mind through awareness training, you can learn to make the necessary shifts. At the end of the day, you have the same mind. It's brilliant and only outputs what you input. It's also capable of changing.

Engage in daily actions to stay focused on achieving your goals, and surround yourself with likeminded individuals. Access resources, such as books and audio recordings, that further reinforce a positive mental attitude. There are times I've played the same audio recording in my car repeatedly for months on end to let my mind deeply absorb the content.

Manifest Your Dreams

These days I also have a notepad at my bedside, so I can write ideas and insights that come to me when I'm working on a goal. I often get ideas when I'm driving.

What have you learned from your journey?

Everyone is here to learn from each other. I hope you can see yourself through my story. Committing to change and learning more about yourself would be a way for you to show self-love and increase your self-worth.

To find out more about me and my programs, including one-to-one coaching sessions, visit my website at www.personalsuccessdevelopment.com.au or find me on Facebook at Personal Success and Development.

> "Nothing is impossible to the mind. All its guidance and power are available to you. When you fully realize that thought causes all, you will know there are never any limits that you yourself do not impose."
> ~Uell Stanley Andersen

To discover more about how Alice can help you *Elevate Your Life*, simply visit www.elevate-books.com/life

Raymond Stapleton

Leveraging Loyalty

Ray Stapleton is a businessman whose focus has always been on the family. In his nearly sixty years in the workforce, he's achieved success in many areas, as well as always being a good provider.

After forging a successful career at the Australia Post, he took early retirement in 1988. Since that time, he's been involved in the taxi industry for over twenty-five years and has also developed and run several vending machines businesses.

Ray is always up for a challenge and is presently rolling out an advertising marketing program for small business. The goal is to create shopping hubs with each participating business supporting each other that has the potential to create a substantial passive income.

Raymond Stapleton
Leveraging Loyalty

What's your biggest life lesson?

Probably the biggest lesson I've learnt in life is to always be yourself and not someone else.

If I go back to my early days, I would have to consider myself lucky. But even though luck does play a part, you do have to play the hand you're dealt.

I was born into a wonderful family, the younger of two boys. My mum and dad were great role models. Our house was nothing outstanding, but I would say our home life was. We didn't have electricity until I was about nine years old. Again, perhaps this was luck, because it meant we had time for each other. We played cards, board games and communicated with each other. Mum and Dad made sure my brother and I were loved and felt special. Or course, this was reciprocal, as we knew our parents were special.

Mum is not someone I'd describe as a person who loved to entertain. She was shy and introverted, but she made sure anyone who visited our home felt welcome and special. Mum saw as her role as making sure our home was the best it could be, while Dad was the provider. We lived out of town on a few acres, and Dad was basically a sheep shearer and rural worker. He didn't have a fancy education, but he had a great work ethic and made sure we were well provided for. We were never rich in a monetary sense, but we never went without, either. So from Dad's example, I learned that to achieve anything, first and foremost, you need a great work ethic.

Another quality I learned from my parents is the importance of being as good as your word, which means having integrity and being honest. When I talk about honesty I don't mean, for example, not taking what isn't yours. That goes without saying. I'm talking about being totally open and honest in everything you do. There were never any hidden agendas with my parents. What you saw was what you got.

What does love mean to you?

I'm somewhat at a loss as to how to put it into words. You hear a lot about love all of the time in songs and in the media. My personal view is that nobody really understands what love is. I believe what people are fed on a daily basis probably gives them a false idea of love.

Regarding my early years growing up and learning from Mum and Dad, I was really describing living with love, as it was everywhere. We didn't often tell those closest to us that we loved them as often as we should, but we certainly all knew it.

My wife and I once attended a marriage enrichment weekend. Upon walking into the conference room, I noticed there were a number of banners on the wall. The first one I saw was *Love is a decision*. My initial reaction was that I'd been conned, since this was supposed to be about enriching my marriage. But by the end of the weekend I realised that love, like most things in life, really is a choice. I can choose to love my wife and family members. Of course, there also may be times when it's necessary to decide not to love someone and move on.

If you were to speak to your younger self, what advice would you give him?

I would say, "Dream big. Back yourself and go for it, but never think you know it all, so never stop learning."

Did you have a big dream when you were younger?

When I was young and at school, I was often accused of being nothing but a dreamer. Sadly, that was true, as I was not the greatest student. I was often guilty of sitting in class and staring out of the window, especially in English class. I would imagine myself walking out at a cricket ground and adjusting the green cap on my head with the Coat of Arms on the front, as I opened the batting for Australia in a Test Match against England.

When one of my early mentors told me I had to get a dream, I struggled with it. I was confusing daydreaming with having a dream. Not that there was anything wrong with my fantasy of playing cricket for Australia, it was just that I didn't have any plan in place to achieve it. Although I did practice hard for a while, at about the age of seventeen I realised girls could be a lot more fun to be with than some of my cricketing mates. That was the end of the fantasy of playing for Australia. I often describe myself as a sporting tragic, since I had to transfer my love of playing it to watching it on TV.

I continued to struggle with the concept of having a dream for quite a while. The turning point for me was when I attended a weekend function at the Rod Laver Arena in Melbourne. The first session was on having a dream. I thought, *Heck, I've come all this way and given up a weekend, and all we're going to hear about is this blasted dream.*

The presenter started out the session by offering $20,000 to anyone who was prepared to walk along a 30cm imaginary plank placed along the front of the stage. Or course, we all stood.

For those who've not been there, The Rod Laver Arena has a high roof. He kept adding imaginary height and asked people to stay standing if they were prepared to do it. I was out of it early, as I'm not good with heights, but many stayed standing right to the top. The presenter then started adding dollars to the equation to get people to stand up again, but I wasn't one of them. In the end, he had us thinking about having the plank from the fortieth story window of one building to another. By this stage he had us all sitting down. But then he added a fire in the other building with one of our children standing at the window. Of course, at this point he had us all standing. I finally understood money wasn't a great motivator, and what he meant by having a dream is that it had to come from emotion.

At the age of fifteen I left school against my parents' wishes, at the completion of what was then called the Intermediate Certificate, which was about the equivalent of the now-defunct NSW School Certificate. At that age, I thought I knew it all and wanted to become a motor mechanic. As an apprentice, I had to service the local farmers' livestock trucks. It's a job I really disliked. In those days, trucks had grease points all over the place, and the farmers always brought them in when it was raining, usually with the livestock carrier still attached, since they weren't able to work on the farm in the rain. As I would crawl underneath, I tried to convince myself the liquid dripping through the wooden floor of the livestock carrier was simply rain water, but in my heart I knew it had more to do with the livestock. After three years, I decided it wasn't for me.

I joined the Postmaster General's Department, which is now known as the Australia Post, and worked as a Postal Clerk in Training. It was then I realised Mum and Dad did know what they were talking about, because in order to gain promotion I needed to complete my high school education, so it was back to night school for me.

Whilst leaving school was a mistake, I did learn a valuable lesson, and that was to be successful in life it takes more than completing one course. So here I am some fifty-six years later, still learning, still attending courses.

Raymond Stapleton

How would you like to be remembered?

For some reason, this is a subject I've often thought about. When you get to my age, sadly you get to attend a lot of funerals, and as a result hear a lot of eulogies, some of which are delivered with great passion by someone who dearly loved the deceased. I've often wondered if when my time comes, whether someone close to me would be able to deliver a eulogy with a passion that would make me proud.

My mum and dad were my heroes, and I recall walking into the one hotel in my hometown shortly after they passed away. There were a number of people there, some I knew and some I didn't, but everyone knew my parents. I was amazed by the amount of people who came up and told me what a privilege it was to have known them both. They talked about how much my parents cared about their community and their friends, and how honest and reliable they were. How they never gossiped or had a bad word to say about anybody. I remember thinking at the time, *Gee, if people can say half as many nice things about me as they did about Mum and Dad, I would be happy.* So I guess that's my goal.

What would you like your legacy to be?

There are two goals in particular I would like to leave as a legacy. The first is to create a business that provides a passive, willable income. Family is, and always has been, extremely important to me, so leaving them an ongoing income stream is first and foremost.

In addition, I've always found it difficult to say no to requests for donations to charities, especially those involving children, and for this reason I would love to set up a foundation with an ongoing income stream.

What is the one message you wish to share with the world?

In Australia we're so lucky. We have so much to be thankful for, but what concerns me is the way people focus on what's wrong rather than what's right. As an example, if a sportsperson goes out to celebrate a mate's birthday and has a few too many drinks, it makes front-page news, but they ignore how many sportspeople do wonderful work with their foundations and charities. Not that I'm condoning misbehaviour or blaming the media, as they have a job to do. I just think the focus is wrong, and the general public should endeavour to change it by refusing to wallow in bad news.

What's the worst thing that's ever happened to you, and how did you overcome it?

At the age of eighteen, after a couple of false starts, I joined Australia Post and was forging ahead with a fairly successful career. Almost thirty years later, I was the manager of a regional country mail centre, and the position was upgraded, so I was required to reapply for my position. For one reason or another, I failed to go up with it. As a result, I was offered a couple of alternatives I deemed unacceptable, and I took a package. It meant giving up a lot, such as a great Super Scheme, and even financial freedom.

Walking out of the office for the last time was tough. I wasn't going to starve overnight, as it was a reasonable package, but I needed a job. My work experience was basically all public sector, twenty-eight years in all, and most of my personal development to that point was job related. At forty-six years of age, with a wife and three children in school, I felt like I'd been thrown on the scrap heap.

But as it turned out, I wasn't out of work for long. Prior to ceasing with Australia Post I'd obtained my licence to drive a cab, so I decided to drive on night shift. Along with my wife, we've now run a taxi business for a number of years and also developed a successful vending machine business, both of which are still running. At present, along with a good friend of ours, we're rolling out a loyalty program for local businesses, and this is where my passion lies at the moment.

Have you had any aha moments that changed everything for you?

Something I believe held me back, especially early in my working life, was my own self-limiting beliefs. I'd convinced myself I couldn't handle public speaking. I was often guilty of sitting at something as simple as a local cricket club meeting, hoping someone would bring up a topic I knew needed to be raised, but I was too fearful to speak up.

The change came for me when Australia Post modified their policy to where post office staff was required to visit local establishments in an effort to regain some of the business lost to courier services, and someone had to train them. My boss, who was a great bloke, asked me to volunteer for the temporary position. I knew if I refused, the one to accept the job would end up in front of me for the next promotion. The position involved a two-week course, and then I had to give some four-day courses for post office staff. At the beginning I was terrified, but by the end I was enjoying it to the point where I was sorry when the job was finished.

So the aha moment for me was when I had the realisation that some of what I'd been telling myself over the years was false. At once I realised I could do so much, provided I set my mind to it.

What decisions have made a difference in your life?

There's little doubt that the decision to volunteer for the temporary position made the utmost difference to my life. Prior to that period, I was restricted in many areas. It opened up more opportunities for me in my career with Australia Post and in my social life, as well as my business career afterward. It was a great boost to my confidence and enabled me to convince myself that other self-limiting beliefs I'd harboured were simply not true. I've continued to take on tasks that at one time I would have talked myself out of doing. For instance, writing this chapter.

For one of my early, but important, promotions with Australia Post, the chairman of the interviewing committee advised me that my wife was the one who deserved the credit for my promotion, as I would probably not have made the short list if I were single. So, making the decision to get married must rate a mention. It probably also means I've said enough about my early life as a young single.

What is your big WHY?

My big WHY is to one day do something for special needs children. It's the one area where I get emotional just thinking about it, and I'm not sure why. Perhaps it goes back to when I was a young man working in the post office at Cowra NSW, and we formed an Ambulance Younger set, where a bunch of us young people would enjoy raising funds to help equip the ambulance station in our town.

In those days, most ambulance drivers were volunteers, and the permanent ambulance officer approached me to train as one. My self-limiting belief kicked in, and I told him no, as I didn't think I could handle it, especially when children were involved. Still, I was almost convinced to give it a try, when I was transferred to Cootamundra. Over the years I've often wondered if I could have made a success of it or not. I think this may be why I've such a passion to help children.

What do you think inspires people?

When I first made the decision to send out my message, I asked myself what was I setting out to achieve, and the word that came to me was *inspire*. I figured if a seventy-four year old could do something he believed was totally impossible, that it may inspire others to start dreaming again. I think many people have had their dreams stolen.

What inspires me is when I see ordinary people achieve extraordinary accomplishments, so I enjoy hearing true stories like that. Actions speak louder than words. For me to be inspired to follow someone, they would need to show me they're committed, authentic and excited.

Why is mindset important?

It took me a long time to realise how powerful the mind can be and how easy it is to sabotage even the best ideas. Perhaps a simple example I could give is by going back to my cricketing days. Over two seasons I got out seven times in a row without making a run, which is called a duck. On the first and second occasions, I was incorrectly given out by the umpire. Of course, I had no say in these decisions.

Where my mindset played a part is that I would walk out to bat thinking, *What silly way will I find to get out today?* It wasn't long before I found out, and usually in an unremarkable way like being clean bowled, which is where the ball touches the wicket without being hit.

I wound up breaking the sequence when I was forced to shift my focus. For the first and only time in my life, I was batting number eleven, a position reserved for the worst batsman in the side, and my batting partner had no idea how to play cricket. My mindset changed to getting on strike as quickly as I could and staying there. Three games later, I was back in first grade as a batsman. This is how I realised I could use my brain to get a positive result instead of sabotaging myself.

How can people be happier in life?

There's no doubt some people wind up in difficult circumstances through no fault of their own. However, I believe many times it's the result of the choices they've made in the past, as well as where they put their focus. One of my teachers in high school told me to remember there's a lot of good in the worst of us, but there's a lot of bad in the best of us. So it's a choice to focus on what you see in people, good or bad. I believe you can choose to focus on the good in the world and your life, rather than what you perceive is the bad, and be much happier for it. This is why I don't watch TV news, as it seems a good story will never get in the way of a bad one.

How can people overcome fear?

There's no doubt fear has held me back over the years. Both fear of failure and fear of what people may think of me. I once thought overcoming fear meant the absence of it, whereas I now believe it's about doing the task despite the fear. One of my mentors said for me to keep two ideas in mind with regard to fear. Generally speaking, people are fearful of something that in all probability isn't going to happen. And as far as what people think of me, he said chances are they won't be thinking of me at all, and that in any event it's none of my business.

Some of what I've found helpful is to focus on what my mentor said about being as well prepared as possible and just doing it anyway. I've heard it said that action cures fear. I'm not sure about that, but it certainly makes life easier.

What's the one thing someone could do right now to change their life?

I would say to be grateful. Over the years, I've been in stressful situations. What I found helpful was to focus on all of the good in my life. My problems seemed less significant, and I was able to focus on moving on. I allowed the Law of Attraction to do its job.

Most people seem to have a natural resistance to change, and it's reinforced with sayings such as, *Better the devil you know*. As a result, they're reluctant to take a risk and try something new.

What's the biggest mistake people make in the area of relationships?

I believe all breakdowns in relationships start and finish with communication, or lack of it. This applies whether it's between husband and wife, family members, friends or business associates.

When two people commit to each other, they generally do so without any formal training. On the other hand, when you decide on a career you often complete a university degree, serve an apprenticeship or receive some form of training. Sadly, in my view a lot of the unsolicited advice given to couples is poor. They'll say marriage is a matter of give and take, or it's a fifty-fifty arrangement. To me, give and take suggests a bargaining arrangement, not a good foundation for a successful relationship. And a fifty-fifty agreement suggests a fifty percent effort. I've never achieved anything when I gave it only half effort.

One major mistake people make is not listening. They're only waiting for the other person to pause, so they can butt in with a reply and wind up misunderstanding what the person was trying to say. I once heard it said that the Good Lord gave us two ears and one mouth, and perhaps that was a hint to listen twice as much as you speak.

Like a lot of people, I thought I was a pretty good communicator, but that all changed when friends of ours suggested we attend the marriage enrichment weekend I mentioned. I soon realised I had a lot to learn about effective communication. It gave me the understanding that a satisfactory relationship can't be maintained without it and not only got me interested in the topic, but self-development in general.

Since that first weekend, I've attended many courses on a variety of subjects and found that good communication is the key to all relationships in every facet of life.

Do you have an approach to building successful business relationships?

In an effort to achieve my goals of providing a willable income for my family and setting up a foundation for special needs children with an ongoing income, I'm presently rolling out a loyalty program as part of my already successful company. It's an advertising marketing program for small businesses.

The initial work consists of a number of steps with opportunities for all who want to participate. The idea is to create local shopping hubs where all involved support each other. It's great for the businesses involved, as it creates fiercely loyal customers. The opportunity is also there to develop an ongoing, passive income for all.

At the outset it requires the business builders, of which I'm one, to establish a relationship with the various local businesses with a view towards them joining the programme. As the shopping hub develops, each business promotes other businesses to their customers that are included in the hub. It's a win for customers, as well as for the businesses.

There's ongoing support provided by both the parent company and leading business builders, by way of regular webinars, training seminars and counselling.

What does success mean to you?

I've been asked this question several times at various courses I've attended, and I used to stress about not being able to define it successfully. I believed if I didn't know what it was, I could never expect to find it.

I once thought of success as a destination, but I now believe it's a journey, and that journey is probably different for everyone. A definition

I came up with, along with the help of my mentor, was that success is the progressive realisation of a worthwhile dream. Of course, the only limits on that dream are the ones you put on it yourself.

What are some common barriers people have to success?

The biggest barrier for me was my own self-limiting belief. As mentioned, I'd convinced myself I couldn't handle public speaking, but there were others. Throughout my schooling and early years, I developed a poor self-image. I always saw my peers as smarter or better than I was, and I really didn't know why. My parents always encouraged me, and I couldn't see any obvious reason to feel the way I did.

It's lucky I attended an intense self-development course, where I was able to explore the reasons for my poor self-image and establish it stemmed from an incident when I was five years old and first starting school. I'm colour blind, so when I was asked to colour in a scene, I had it all wrong. The teacher used my scene as an example to my peers of how not to do it. As a consequence, I judged myself as inferior and reinforced this opinion of myself many times over the years.

The course I attended was good for me, because I discovered I wasn't the only one who made life-changing decisions at an early age. In fact, most people do. Once I became aware of this, I was able to work on myself and take on tasks I wouldn't otherwise have done. I feel sad when I hear many people doing exactly what I did. Often when I've presented an opportunity to someone, I get responses like, "I could never do that" or "That's just not me."

Do you have a coach, mentor or someone who motivates you?

Over the years I've had several coaches, especially when taking on tasks where I'm out of my comfort zone. I think it's important when selecting a coach to make sure they've achieved the level you're trying to accomplish and not someone who just talks the talk. People are keen to give unsolicited advice that amounts to nothing more than opinion, and from my experience, opinions are not often helpful.

How do they make a difference to your success?

Regarding my business, most of the work I do is establishing a relationship with businesspeople in our area, and whilst that's something I've been interested in for many years, I know I have a lot I need to learn and obstacles to overcome. Without a mentor, I tend to become frustrated, procrastinate and finally stop altogether.

What do you believe keeps people in a job they dislike, and what holds them back from achieving the lifestyle they desire?

Self-limiting beliefs and confidence in their own ability. They convince themselves they're not good enough to try something else, and therefore it's futile to take the necessary action to make a change.

People are too afraid to make big decisions and wind up in a job or business that's not fulfilling and simply stick it out, while convincing themselves it's the best option, because it's secure and something they know. On the other hand, if you're prepared to embrace change and take some risks, the situation could be a lot different.

What can you give as the best steps to success?

To be truly successful I believe, first and foremost, that you must do something you enjoy or are passionate about. You've probably heard the expression, *Find something you love doing and never work a day in your life*. As a general rule, I've enjoyed my work. When I was fifteen, I was convinced I wanted to become a motor mechanic, but I soon realised I didn't enjoy it, and as a result was not going to be successful. On the other hand, when I joined Australia Post and later wound up running my own business, I found them both enjoyable, and as a result

I succeeded. The common thread in each career choice I've made was interacting with people and serving them to the best of my ability. I've always obtained great job satisfaction when I'm able to help someone by providing an excellent service or product.

Of course, there's more to success than just finding something you like doing. I've often seen people reach a certain level, and as if by magic they seem to think they know it all, which leads to disastrous results, such as cutting off vital information or not seeking specialist advice where necessary.

You will need to be committed to your cause and persevere, as circumstances won't always simply fall into place. You must also have integrity, a good work ethic, do that little bit extra, and be prepared to listen and learn.

 To discover more about how Ray can help you *Elevate Your Life*, simply visit

www.elevate-books.com/life

Rebekah Smith
Elevate Your Energy

Rebekah Smith is a physiotherapist, fitness professional and wellbeing consultant. She's dedicated the last fifteen years of her life to understanding and working with the human body and psyche. Her unique approach to work and life revolves around her deep understanding of both scientific and spiritual principles.

Bek is an accomplished clinician who acts as a mentor and trainer, an Australian fitness leader sponsored by a global brand, and a parent who's determined for shaping the best world possible for her family and community.

Inspired by the work of Eckhart Tolle, Susan Cain, Tristan Taormino, Brené Brown and Martin Seligman, Bek describes herself as an introverted optimist with a special interest in sexual wellbeing and bioelectricity.

Rebekah Smith

Elevate Your Energy

How did you become interested in health and wellbeing?

I've always had a fascination with biology and a love of performing. I was a high achiever in science and drama at school, which some people say is an unusual combination, but I just loved learning about different ways to use the body and mind. For me, science always seemed to hold the answers for how everyone fits into the bigger picture of the world, and the performing arts were a way for me to express the wonder I felt about it.

As I progressed from childhood into adolescence, I experienced a series of events that made me question my worthiness and feel a sense of fear and shame about expressing myself. I became more and more self-conscious and inhibited and felt like I would never live up to others' expectations, or even my own. It became easy to withdraw into my textbooks and be a science nerd, rather than putting myself out there on display as a performance artist.

I quietly finished high school before getting a science degree while staying under the radar, so nobody would notice how imperfect I was. During my studies I majored in psychology and human physiology, which deepened my interest and understanding of what makes humans tick. Then it came time to use my knowledge and attempt to make a difference out in the big, wide world. I started off in research, hoping I'd make amazing discoveries that would help all of humankind, and with any luck also stay anonymous and unacknowledged in case I made any embarrassing mistakes. I was surprised to discover I was deeply unfulfilled by my work and started seeking a new way of being.

I left my job, went back to university research and published a scientific paper. Then I decided I wanted to work out in the field with people, instead of in a science lab. I also needed a way to use both my physical and intellectual abilities, so I started teaching group fitness. It paid my way through another degree as I studied physiotherapy. That's when I realised I'd come full circle. The applied science of physio satisfied my craving to keep learning more about physiology and psychology, and my work as a fitness instructor gave me a licence to perform in front of people again. For the first time since childhood, I felt like I could express my natural talents and interests in a way that made me feel valuable, whilst also helping other people.

What inspires you to lend your skills and knowledge to helping others?

I believe fulfilment in life is directly related to your connections, and that helping others is one of the best ways of developing a connection. I also feel extremely grateful for the opportunities I've had, and I feel a sense of duty to share what I've gained. I'm always happy to share my knowledge, experiences and passions.

I've had a number of teachers and mentors who've lent me their time, wisdom and care for no other reason than to help me become a better person. I may never be able to return the favour directly, so I pay it forward and hope it creates a ripple effect of positive energy.

How do you use your past experiences to make a difference in people's lives?

I embrace both the positive and the negative, which I believe is pivotal. Rather than concealing or hiding from the dark patches of my past, I consider every experience a learning opportunity for myself and others. I don't mind sharing moments of pain and vulnerability if it will help somebody gain a different perspective or understanding.

I make a difference by educating, being compassionate and connecting people with each other, their own inner wisdom, and the world around them. I believe everyone is biologically hardwired to connect, because we're all linked to a common energetic field. My past experiences have definitely helped me understand this.

Could you expand on the experiences that have shaped the work you do today?

It's taken me a long time to put those pieces together for myself! It was only recently I realised there's one common factor between everything I'm passionate about, and that's the use of energy. The work I do is all about bioelectricity, or how energy flows within and between living organisms. I see bioelectricity as the foundation of life itself, and a balanced bioelectrical system means optimal quality of life.

Many factors influence energy flow, not the least of which are cognition and psychological processing. As I mentioned, I've always been interested in what makes people tick, so I absolutely love learning about psychology.

But on a professional level I avoided becoming a clinical psychologist, because I was concerned about being drawn into the negativity bias, which is the evolutionary tendency of the human brain to focus on the negative. This is useful for survival when you need to be on the lookout for threats, but in everyday life it's the cause of a great deal of anxiety and depression. For that reason I turned away from working with a problem-focussed lens and moved towards positive psychology, a field dedicated to helping people thrive and flourish. As a wellness coach, I use the uplifting work of Martin Seligman, Chris Peterson, Tal Ben-Shahar and Megan McDonough to rewire the nervous system so that energy flows more through the circuits people use for connection, meaning and love, thereby turning the focus away from suffering and towards joyful living.

Another way I've learnt to alleviate suffering and improve energy flow is through neurodynamics, which is my favourite area of physiotherapy work. This approach addresses how different parts of the nervous system function and communicate with each other and the rest of the body. Many people don't realise their nerves can wind up mechanically restricted, just as their muscles can become tight and shortened. In fact, many of the muscular and joint issues people use massage or therapy for have an underlying neurodynamic problem as well. Unfortunately, many musculoskeletal therapists don't treat the neurodynamic issues directly, and their clients continue to have recurrent problems. My experience in helping people with their physical channels of energy has been enormously satisfying and is one of the few physiotherapy treatments I still perform.

My work as a fitness instructor has also helped me appreciate the importance of bioelectricity. Aside from the obvious physical benefits, exercise has a way of balancing a person mentally and connecting them with others through energy shifts and exchanges. After years in the fitness industry, I've come to realise this is probably the most valuable part of group exercise, and I see it particularly in dance and mind-body classes such as yoga and Pilates. These classes have a way of helping people focus inwardly, become more mindful, while also letting go of the inhibitions society, and past experiences, have placed on them. I just love seeing people lose themselves in music and movement and feel absolutely privileged they allow me to join them in that experience.

In short, my professional life has helped me understand everyone is connected, and if connections can be enhanced by optimising flow across all areas, you elevate your life.

Have your personal experiences influenced your work?

Yes, definitely. There are two areas I love working in, and each of them has a backstory. Warning: the first story may contain emotional triggers for some readers.

One of my darker moments occurred when I was a teenager and had a huge crush on a boy at school. During a party, I was thrilled to find myself in a tight embrace with him, kissing in a quiet spot, when all of a sudden it turned into a non-consensual sexual experience. My reaction at the time was to freeze, and afterwards I acted as if nothing happened. It was a secret I held onto for years, because of the deep sense of shame and embarrassment I felt about it. There were so many questions I couldn't answer for myself. Why did I freeze? Why hadn't I said or done anything? How could I have been stupid enough to put myself in that situation? The shame festered inside of me for a long time and only started to ease once I talked about what happened and shared it with people close to me.

This experience forever coloured my views about sex, but perhaps not in the negative way you might expect. After sharing my story and learning to accept it, I became curious about the dynamics around how it had occurred, what conditions allowed it to happen, and how these factors influence sexuality in society. I did mention I'm a big nerd, right?

I realised that as far as my negative experience was concerned, neither the boy nor I were to blame. I hadn't felt comfortable in expressing what I wanted and expected from the situation, and neither had he. In his naivety, he probably believed my interest in him was consent enough, and I hadn't offered any information to make him believe otherwise. The strong, underlying message I took from all of this is that sex happens, but it's not talked about enough, so the end result is that people don't experience it on good terms. It's wrapped in such a cloak of shame and embarrassment they tiptoe around it most of the time, which only makes the situation worse.

I decided I wanted to bring more discussion about sex out into the open, which is why I now run group workshops, couples sessions and individual education about sexual wellbeing. My hope is that by removing the stigma surrounding sex, it will decrease sexual violence and improve people's enjoyment of this important aspect of life.

What's the story behind your interest in spirituality, and how does this fall under the umbrella of bioelectricity?

The other area of work and study I find endlessly fascinating is based around the integration of science and spirituality. Up until I was in my early twenties, I was a hard-headed fan of the scientific method. I advocated evidence-based approaches and believed that if it couldn't be measured, it didn't exist. Then I met one of my best friends, who I now call my spiritual brother, and an experience I had with him shook the very foundations of my beliefs.

When we met, I experienced a connection that made me feel like I'd known him my whole life. We became friends and then housemates rather quickly, and the extra time spent together seemed to strengthen our bond. One day when I was at university, I came down with a sudden and severe migraine, accompanied by nausea and vomiting. I'd never even been a headache sufferer, so this was unusual for me. The worst part was the simultaneous feeling of pure dread that came with it.

I struggled home and described the sensations to my friend: intense pain, illness and this sense of impending doom I couldn't shake. I confided in him that I felt like something awful was going to happen to somebody I cared about. He told me to think positive and rest up, and then I took the afternoon off to recover and returned to uni the next day.

In between lectures I noticed I'd a missed call from my friend. I called him back, and his voice told me he was shaken. He said, "Bek, it wasn't you... that feeling you had yesterday was a message for me. I just found out a friend of mine has died."

You could have knocked me over with a feather. That day the sceptic in me took a permanent holiday. If I'd heard that story from somebody else, I would have written it off as coincidence. Having personally experienced those thoughts and that deep sense of knowing something was amiss, diverted my scientific mind towards new lines of enquiry. I became just as curious about what can't be measured as what can. These days I love working with topics other health professionals find too difficult, such as nerve impulses, emotions and the way the human body and psyche interact. This is why I now consider myself a bioelectrician who tests, measures and improves the unseen energy flow of human systems.

What is your concept of spirituality, and how does it tie into your approach?

For me, spirituality is all about connection, love and faith in the unknown. This quote from Brené Brown beautifully sums up my view: "Spirituality is recognizing and celebrating that we are all inextricably connected to each other by a power greater than all of us, and that our connection to that power and to one another is grounded in love and compassion. Practicing spirituality brings a sense of perspective, meaning and purpose to our lives." Some people call the greater power *God*, some call it *nature* and some call it *source energy*. I tend to refer to it as *the universe* or *the energy field*.

One of the reasons I've come to believe so strongly in spiritual concepts is because I now understand science is only as good as its instruments, and they're still constantly improving. How arrogant I was in my younger years, thinking that only the tangible was worth studying? After all, dogs hear frequencies of sound humans can't, and light exists in wavelengths that can't be detected with the human eye. Think about a time when Galileo was considered crazy for suggesting the world was round, penicillin was unknown and people would have believed the simplest use of electricity was witchcraft. What currently unknown concepts will be common knowledge in a hundred years?

My approach is now based on the belief that if a theory hasn't been proven, maybe it just hasn't been proven *yet*. I still have a great deal of respect for science. I simply recognise it doesn't have all of the answers *right now*. Herein lays the basis for my work. As a student and teacher of bioelectricity, I recognise that every molecule, every atom, every particle in existence, vibrates at a particular frequency. When energy is transformed from one place or form to another, the particles involved change in vibration. Large shifts in energy are obvious, like an electric potential that can be measured in volts, but smaller shifts can cause a vibration change so subtle there are no instruments to measure them.

I work with energy changes that can be scientifically detected, while also appreciating there will be other shifts I can't measure. It's my belief that spirituality is merely a pointer to what science hasn't been able to measure, and perhaps never will.

What are the forms of bioelectricity you can measure?

Apart from neurodynamic work, my main mode of scientific enquiry with my clients is through heart rate variability. It's quick to measure, non-invasive and easy to understand, so people can relate to it. This method also has a large number of applications.

Heart rate variability, or HRV, has been studied since the 1700s and much more extensively since the 1960s as technology has progressed. Studies show the heart contains a lot more information than merely how fast or slow it beats. Fluctuations in heart rate provide information about how other body systems work. The majority of evidence collected shows that poor HRV is related to life-threatening disease processes like diabetes, liver cirrhosis and cardiovascular disease, as well as being implicated in chronic fatigue syndrome, fibromyalgia, depression, anxiety and irritable bowel syndrome. It's a marker for biological aging and can detect which people in certain patient groups are most likely to die from their condition and who will recover.

How is heart rate variability related to such a wide range of problems?

The link is the autonomic nervous system. In the human body, the nervous system is divided into branches according to function. The central nervous system (CNS) is made up of the brain and spinal cord, and the peripheral nervous system (PNS) is made up of nerves that connect the rest of the body back to the CNS.

The PNS itself is divided into three parts: the somatic nervous system supplies the muscles, joints and skin, the autonomic nervous system (ANS) supplies the internal organs, blood vessels and glands, and the enteric nervous system (ENS) supplies the gastrointestinal tract. The ENS was once considered part of the ANS, as they're strongly linked, but it's now classified as a system in its own right. The outline below shows the two branches of the ANS, the sympathetic and parasympathetic nervous systems, which together determine heart rate variability.

1) CENTRAL NERVOUS SYSTEM (brain, spinal cord)

2) PERIPHERAL NERVOUS SYSTEM (nerves outside of the CNS)

    a. SOMATIC (muscles, joints, skin)

    b. ENTERIC (gut)

    c. AUTONOMIC (internal organs, blood vessels, glands)

        i. SYMPATHETIC NERVOUS SYSTEM

        ii. PARASYMPATHETIC NERVOUS SYSTEM

Heart rate variability is a useful measure, because it shows what the autonomic nervous system is doing. The heart is just one of the many organs supplied by the ANS but the easiest to get information from. Heart function is analysed to check whether the sympathetic and parasympathetic nervous systems are working together or are imbalanced. In a world full of stress, most people are out of balance without realising it. They have no awareness of what their nervous system chaos is doing to them. This is a fundamental issue in many states of disease and stress but one that's largely overlooked.

How do these nervous system imbalances affect people?

The sympathetic nervous system (SNS) is responsible for the flight-or-fight response and is activated during times of stress when energy is needed to flee from danger or fight for your life. The characteristic signs of the SNS response are a racing heart, increased sweating and feeling hot and flushed. You also feel like your stomach is tied in knots. This is because blood flow decreases to the gut and diverts to the muscles, making you better able to run and less able to digest, which is the last thing your body needs to spend energy on if you're running for your life.

If you've ever been really nervous, you'll recognise these symptoms. That's because the threat detector in your brain interprets incidents like public speaking and embarrassing moments as actual scary and dangerous situations, so it triggers the SNS to activate. I go more in-depth on this topic in my workshops and courses.

The parasympathetic nervous system (PSNS), on the other hand, is responsible for what happens during rest, relaxation and recovery. It's referred to as the rest-and-digest response or sometimes *feed-and-breed*. PSNS activation slows down the heart rate, lowers blood pressure, increases blood supply to the gut and controls digestion. It's also responsible for sexual arousal. You can probably understand why an imbalance between the SNS and PSNS causes blood pressure issues, digestive complaints and lack of sexual drive or performance, amongst many other issues.

An analogy I heard perfectly describes their function and impact. If your system were a vehicle, think of the SNS as your accelerator and the PSNS as your brake. In order for your vehicle to move well and last a long time, you need to have smooth fluctuations between the brake and accelerator at appropriate times. What happens if you try to use both pedals at the same time or stomp on them haphazardly? It leads to more wear and tear on your vehicle and a pretty rough ride. Yet this is what so many people do every day without realising it. Various parts break down, leading to injuries and illnesses that seem to come out of nowhere. The ride of life becomes bumpy and unenjoyable, and your mental health takes a downward turn. Yet because you may not understand bioelectricity and the role of your nerves on your wellbeing, the cause of your suffering could remain a mystery.

Why do these imbalances occur, and what can people do about them?

There are a great number of factors that affect nervous system balance, but all of them share a common factor: stress. Maybe it's a certain food, a lack of exercise or even over-exercising that weakens the system. Maybe it's drug or alcohol use, financial hardship, poor sleep, relationship problems or being miserable at work. Whatever the stressor, every one of them leads to overactivity of the sympathetic nervous system and inhibits the parasympathetic response.

Unfortunately, you can't always change your circumstances, and in the world we live in there's no way you can free yourself from every stressor. What you can do is learn how to respond to stress differently. This is both a psychological and a physiological effort, and again, there's a common factor. If stress, illness and suffering are mediated through the SNS, the solution is to strengthen the PSNS. In fact, you'll discover that every healing modality, every stress-relief system and every valid solution to a life problem is designed, intentionally or inadvertently, to activate the parasympathetic nerves and settle the flight-or-fight response.

What is your system for helping people better respond to stress?

I take a step-by-step approach with my clients, guiding them through the three areas they can work on to optimise their bioelectrical function. Each area is deeply connected to the others, and each solution has balance as its aim. The three problem areas, and the common issues I help people overcome, are shown in this diagram:

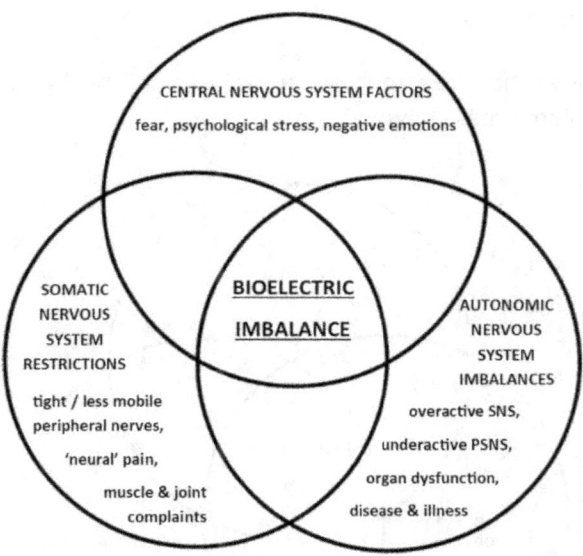

There are many different approaches that can be taken to address each of the issues outlined above, such as psychology, counselling, physical therapy, medication and meditation. The list is long, and the effectiveness of each varies from person to person. The take-home message I want to emphasize is that unless you address every problem area, an issue in one area will eventually spill over into the others. You can work on your physical health as much as you like, but if negative emotion dominates your life, your central nervous system will eventually poison your somatic and autonomic systems to produce pain and illness. Ignoring your neurodynamics, stress or niggling recurrent illnesses, means the issue will show up somewhere via the interrelated nervous system, and not always in the place you might expect.

This all happens because of connection. Nothing in the universe, let alone the human body, functions in isolation away from everything else. It's time people stopped treating themselves as a collection of separate parts and start to appreciate the amazing wholeness they are, and are a part of.

Have a look at the three approaches I take to holistically address each of the problem areas shown above:

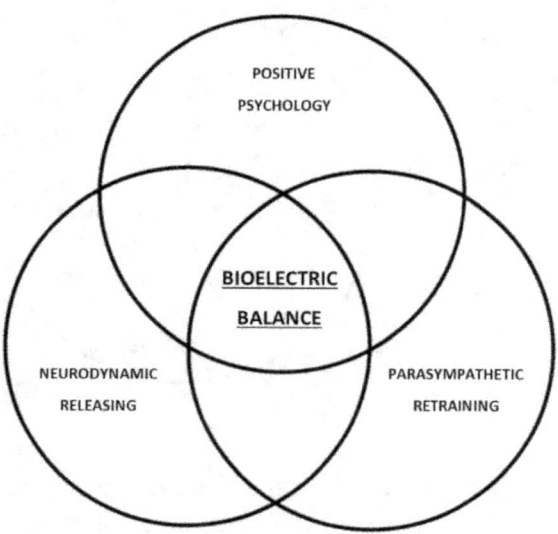

Each of these approaches requires active participation on the part of the person seeking change. This is not a treatment for the passive or a quick-fix system. Coaching using positive psychology models is a gradual process requiring consistent practice. Neurodynamic releasing can't be done all at once and is necessarily performed slowly and gently. Parasympathetic retraining involves heart rate biofeedback, which requires time and concentration. However, the benefits of slow and gradual change are enormous, as the rewiring of the nervous system is robust, and the resultant positive changes in energy flow are long-lasting.

How do you deliver your solutions for stress and help people elevate their energy?

I'm open with my clients, and the first question I ask is if they're actually ready for change. I'm happy to be a facilitator by teaching people new information and explaining the process they need to take, but I can't *fix* anyone. I believe strongly in taking accountability and being responsible for one's own behaviours and choices. If somebody is genuinely ready to change for the better, I have many paths that can elevate them, and I'll work with them on a one-to-one basis, as a couple, family, or in small groups. I offer consultation for small working teams, as well as bigger corporate groups, and also educate through public speaking to large audiences. My sessions range from informative seminars, interactive workshops and short courses, right through to getaway retreats for a more immersive experience.

After years of doing individual consultation, these days I do prefer group coaching and education for two reasons: I can get my message out to more people, and the group effect is powerful. Not only does it stimulate more discussion and greater learning, but it develops a sense of rapport and community between people, just like I see in my fitness classes. At the end of the day, everything I do is about connection, so one of the best parts about group work is being able to connect people with one another. There's some interesting research being done about how the electromagnetic fields of bodies interact to facilitate connection and non-verbal communication between people, which I discuss in my HRV education sessions.

Whatever the delivery method, my goal is always to help people reach a deep level of understanding, and that doesn't happen simply by giving information. There are a lot of great facts, figures and informative tidbits out there, coming at you with unprecedented speed thanks to technology, but you don't always have someone guiding you in how to filter and then *use* that information. I have three stages I like to take people through to elicit real and lasting change: *Learn, Integrate* and *Apply*, otherwise known as the LIA methodology.

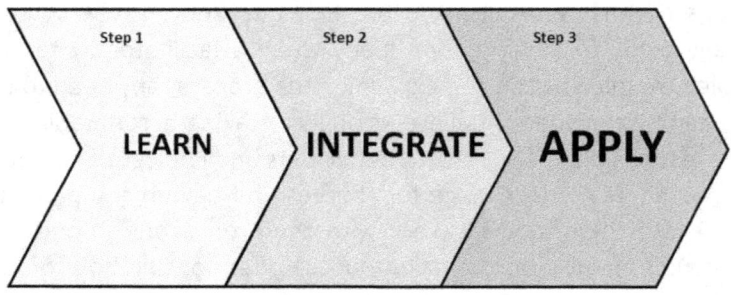

Learning new information is easy, but putting it into practice requires more time, a different level of nervous system processing and a more committed approach. The learning stage is what I cover in my speaking events. The integration phase occurs through practice workshops, and the real-life application happens in between contact with my clients. The beauty of this process is that when I run a follow-up workshop, a debriefing session or simply progress through a course, everyone gets to touch base with one another, talk about what worked and what didn't and fine tune the next steps in order to keep moving forward together. In group sessions the participants get to know each other, form friendships based on support and feel they're taking a journey together instead of going it alone. Growing and progressing as a collective is a wonderful way of practicing and receiving compassion, community development and even nurturing unity in the world. I think everyone should do more of it.

What's your final word on how people can elevate their energy for greater health, happiness and success?

One of the best pieces of advice I can offer is that true greatness happens *outside* of your comfort zone. I don't mean you should do what makes you miserable. Quite the opposite. Do what challenges you and makes you nervous. Do what you didn't think you could, so you end up stronger, happier and more confident. When I look back on my life so far, I can say the most difficult experiences have opened doors and rewarded me with the greatest outcomes. I do believe you need to be willing to lean into discomfort to experience the kind of growth that makes up an enriched life. On a bioelectrical level, when you experience discomfort followed by relief and achievement, it synchronises your nervous system and also resets your tolerance threshold, making you better able to cope with greater challenges later if you need to. This is how people become more resilient human beings.

Lastly, I'm happy to share with you three philosophies I live my life by. The first I've kept in mind since I was a kid. When people asked me what I wanted to do when I grew up, I always thought, and sometimes said, that I just wanted to wake up in the morning and look forward to what I was doing that day. I'm proud to say I've done pretty well with that.

The second is a question I ask myself regularly. *If I were to die right now from some terrible stroke of luck, would I be satisfied I spent my time well?* That always helps me keep life in perspective and my priorities in order, so I can decide how best to channel my energy.

The third is my view on success, which I define in energetic, rather than material, terms. Somebody who knows me quite well once gave me a wall-hanging with a Buddhist quote: *Success is not the key to happiness. Happiness is the key to success. If you love what you are doing, you will be successful.* Every time I walk past it, I smile and am reminded to stay on track and follow my passions.

Here's to you following yours!

 To discover more about how Bek can help you *Elevate Your Life*, simply visit www.elevate-books.com/life

Summer SJ Ng

Love and Connection

Summer SJ Ng is a dedicated author and founder of Freedom to Be, an organization that helps women realise their Power within, to achieve their wildest dreams and be their own hero. She was a CPA member for ten years and is a certified self-defence instructor.

She's passionate about helping others live a life they love and love the life they live. Her ability to listen and tune in to her clients gives them the freedom to explore their options without judgment. Clients gain clarity and insights as she prompts and leads them through powerful, effective questioning and processes to help them discover their own answers to life's challenges.

Summer brings a beautiful flow to the journey she guides her clients through, helping them relax and find solutions to the complex and complicated issues they face.

Summer SJ Ng

Love and Connection

What's your biggest life lesson?

I had to learn I'm worthy of having an amazing, beautiful, creative and expansive human experience, and that life is filled with adventures and fun.

Of course, life has ups and downs, just like a rollercoaster. I choose to ride with both arms in the air, squealing in delight, because I'm having so much fun. Art Linkletter said, "Things turn out best for the people who make the best out of the way things turn out." The highs and lows, the twists and turns, exist in order for me to experience all of the aspects of this wonderful, breathtaking journey called life.

As you become more aware of who you are, exploring and breaking through perceived limitations and learning you're a powerful, magnificent and creative being, you expand and create ripple effects.

If you were speaking to your younger self, what advice would you give?

I would look her in the eyes and say with a gentle smile:

"Dearest, darling, most beautiful, loveable Summer, YOU ARE WORTHY just because you exist. You are seen. You are heard. You are loved. You matter.

Do what you feel called to do. Take that chance, and see where it leads. Trust your inspiration. It will always pay off. There's no need to be afraid. Life is always working out for you. Trust yourself and your inner voice. Tune in, listen and heed what it says. You hold the answers to what you seek.

Love and Connection

Pay attention to how you feel. Do more of what makes you feel good.

Be present. Life is in the here and now. All is well.

You always have a choice. You are a powerful creator. You can have everything your heart desires. What you appreciate in life, appreciates.

When you change the way you look at people and situations, the people and situations you look at will change.

Life is fun, easy and full of possibilities. It really is just a game. You're safe to explore and play, so go and have as many adventures as you like.

When something or someone stops being fun, good for you, or a joyful endeavour, you're allowed to walk away with no guilt, shame, fear or judgment.

Appreciate the contrasts in life. They give you clarity, so you can adjust and realign yourself to your desires. Variety is the spice of Life. "

Then I would give her a long, tight hug, so she felt embraced in love.

What does love mean to you?

To me, love equals the freedom to be your authentic self and express your inner truths without any fear, guilt, shame or self-judgment. It means evolving and having the freedom to play and explore, to stay or go. Love also means being kind, gentle, and passionate, while having appreciation, compassion, honesty, openness and courage.

Love means having awareness and paying attention by giving full acceptance, while allowing yourself to be who you are and do what makes you happy and lights you up.

There's a saying that goes, *Live and let live*. I like to think of love as *Be and let be*. To me, loving someone means being your truest, most real self without pretence, while allowing the ones you love to be their most authentic selves and consciously choosing to be with them, even if it's just in spirit.

What's the worst thing that's ever happened to *you*, and how did *you* overcome *it*?

The worst thing that's ever happened to me was experiencing sexual abuse when I was a teen. I judged myself harshly for it and felt ashamed and guilty. I thought I was to blame. That somehow I was responsible. I kept it from family and friends, petrified of what would happen if I told them the truth. I was so terrified of bringing disgrace to my family and being scorned. I despised myself and felt disgusted, like I was used and damaged goods.

I felt powerless and not worth a single cent. My self-confidence plummeted, my grades started to suffer, and later on as a young adult, this deep-seated feeling of unworthiness led to me having and staying in a toxic, abusive relationship for eight years.

Alongside feeling stressed out and tired most of the time, I was unhappy and withdrew into myself. I was angry, hurt, frustrated and so sad, lonely and confused. My relationship with my family and friends became strained, until it finally came to a point where I felt I didn't recognize myself anymore, and it wasn't safe to be me. I felt that even though I was doing my best, it was never good enough. I was never good enough.

I was constantly in conflict within myself. A part of me knew something was wrong and that I needed to leave the relationship, while another part of me couldn't see a future where "someone better" would appreciate and love me for who I was.

Love and Connection

I feel that the end of my toxic relationship was really when I started to learn who I was. That I *am* worthy. That I've always had, and still have, my personal power. I didn't understand the impact of my experiences until I had my heart broken into what felt like a million pieces and had to look for ways to rebuild my life and fill that gaping void. I began to ask myself, *Who am I? How can I be happy? How do I feel whole again?* and searched hard for the answers to those questions.

I was desperate to know how I could feel safe, have peace and stop feeling so sad. I just wanted to be happy. Somehow, I sensed there was a joyful being at my core, and I needed to learn how I could be the person I wanted to be.

I discovered books and teachers who taught about self-love and self-worth, and I started reading and studying how to nurture, care for and love myself. How to be kind and gentle towards myself while remembering I'm always doing the best I can in each moment.

I poured my thoughts and emotions into my journals, allowing my tears to flow freely, and I came to realise which of my closest friends understood what I was going through and would lend me their ears and a shoulder to cry on.

I subscribed to newsletters, read books, saw a counsellor, and attended webinars and online courses. I did the work I had to do, felt called to do, in order to learn about myself and to heal my wounds. One of my favourite exercises is Louise Hay's Mirror Work. It sounded so simple. You look in a mirror and say, "I love you." It was really challenging at first! I felt so uncomfortable and weird looking into my own eyes for the first time. I managed to hold my own gaze and squeak like a mouse, "I like you." Gradually, it became easier with practice. I'm so grateful I persevered with the exercise. I still remember the moment of being awash by emotion as I said, heard and felt the words, "I love you."

It's powerful, and so important, to be seen, heard and feel loved by someone, even if that someone is you. In fact, I believe it's important that it does include you. I learnt to soothe and hug myself and to look inwards and realise I'm in control of how I choose to live my life. As Dr. Wayne Dyer said, "Change your thoughts, change your life."

This is a continuous journey of self-discovery and self-actualization. Attending Authentic Education's Turning Point Intensive Weekend in January 2015 was one of the major turning points in my life. I'm deeply grateful to Benjamin J Harvey, Cham Tang and their team for being who they are and doing the work they do.

Through Ben's teachings, I've learnt to overcome even more of the shame, guilt, fear and judgment I was carrying. Some of it I hadn't even been aware of before. Today, I'm embracing and loving myself more than ever and continue to take inspired action by doing what I love.

I experienced my own transformation and have seen firsthand many lives change for the better. I know you can do it as well. I continue to refine my skills to be of even greater service and gain great pleasure and satisfaction in guiding others to find the happiness, fulfilment, success and love they desire and deserve.

What's the one message you wish to share with the world?

We are all one and connected. The answers you seek lie within you. Shed what's untrue of you. Learn who you truly are, be who you really are, and love all of who you are. If you do, you'll understand others at their core and accept and love them for who they are.

Have you had any aha moments that changed everything for you?

One of my major *aha* moments was realising it was up to me to change my life and give myself the happiness and fulfilment I seek. That's my responsibility, nobody else's. I hold the power and freedom to live my life how I want to, as long as it's safe for me and others, and safe for the planet. I am worthy, just because I exist. I really am safe, and this is all just a game, so I can play as big as I want to my heart's content.

The moment I hit rock bottom, I knew nothing else would hurt me that bad. The only direction was *up*. All of this inspires me to continually work on building a life I love and desire and to do what's meaningful, purposeful, and fulfilling to me.

What decisions have you made that created a difference in your life?

The moment I decided I'd had enough of being abused and deserved way more than what I was getting. I ended my unhealthy relationship and resigned from a job that was no longer meaningful. Afterwards, I fulfilled a long-term dream and bought myself a one-way ticket for my first solo trip to Europe.

I made a decision to treat myself right, with the knowledge that we teach others how to treat us. From that point on I watched my relationships shift as I began to show up for myself in a different way, and raised the bar for what was acceptable behaviour and what wasn't. I gave myself permission to say no to people and walk away when required. I learnt to communicate my needs instead of shove them aside.

I also decided that my life is *now*. I choose to no longer be afraid of giving myself what I desire. Each time I decide to back myself, even when it seems like I don't have the resources, somehow the universe delivers, and the situation works out in my best interest.

What's the best thing that's ever happened to you and why?

The best thing that's ever happened to me is having been put on this planet in the family I have, being alive right now, feeling each breath and having the experiences I've had. Each moment in my life has led to the next and brought me to the here and now, knowing what I know and feeling how I feel. I'm deeply grateful and appreciative for this human experience and am excited to see what else is coming my way.

Everything I've been through has helped me experience so many contrasts. If any of it were missing, my life at this point would probably be completely different. I have no regrets about my past, and I'm creating my future now.

What do you believe you've been put on the planet to do?

I believe I'm here to serve, connect, love, expand, learn, and have fun!

How are you currently making a difference in people's lives?

By being myself and sharing passionately and humbly about what I love, know and am learning. When I'm interested and curious about people, I'm connecting from my heart and making a difference through coaching and empowering them.

A great way to make a difference is to simply listen. At the end of the day, people want to feel heard, seen and understood. Often in articulating thoughts and emotions, people come to their own *aha* moments and realisations and find their own solutions to the challenges they face.

My role is to hold a safe space for people to release any fear, guilt, shame or self-judgment. They can relax and be themselves and explore. Together, we delve as deeply as they would like to. If a goal seems too big, I can help break it down and take the smallest step required in heading towards the goal. If someone needs their hand held, then I would gladly do it. There are limitless possibilities as to what people can do.

I'm here to support and encourage people and hold them accountable when required. In this way they can get to where they want to go, while they enjoy the journey.

What are you passionate about?

I'm passionate about helping people realise the freedom they have to be whoever they want to and unfold into who they truly are, in order to have everything their heart desires. I'm on their team to help them realise their personal power and turn their dreams into reality. This fulfils my own values for connection and intimacy, growth and development.

It's such a privilege and a humbling experience to be able to create a safe space for people and witness their transformation . I'm deeply grateful to be given that trust and to share in their journey.

What do you think people's biggest life issues are?

I think one of the biggest issues people tend to have is worrying about what other people think of and expect from them. They live their lives the way they *think* others expect them to, instead of learning to self-love and allowing themselves to live the life they want, doing what they love and playing by their own rules.

What do you want out of your life? Have you asked yourself that before? If you know what you want, what's been stopping you from achieving it? Are you waiting for permission from someone else in order to reach for your dreams?

Especially during childhood, you're taught to believe certain concepts that are simply untrue. You're taught to feel guilt, shame and fear around parts of yourself, and you begin to keep secrets, hiding those shameful parts away. Then as an adult, your interpretation of certain situations might be faulty based on the beliefs you've learned and experiences you've had. This can add up and weigh so heavily on you, that you get physical symptoms of this stress via disease.

The good news is that when you gain courage, shed what's untrue and expose your secrets, you begin to feel happier, lighter and better. Your body also starts to return to a state of ease.

What's the best way to help people with this issue?

I feel the best way to help is to educate them.

There comes a point when you learn you don't need external permission to live the life you want. What you need is internal allowance. This means it's important to give yourself permission to have what you want and be who you are meant to be. Then you open the possibility to discover how to achieve your desires and live a happy, fulfilled and meaningful life.

What's your approach to life?

My approach to life is a simple-seven-step system called FREEDOM.

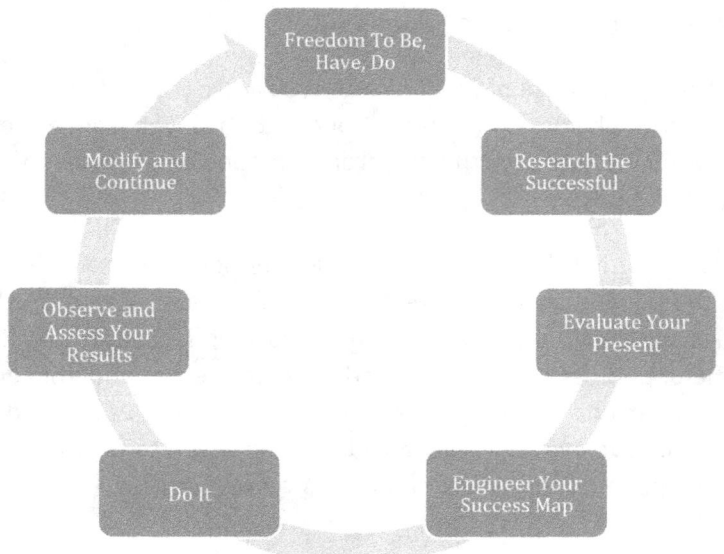

The FREEDOM Seven-Step System

Step 1: Freedom to Be, Have, Do

The first step is to do your best to free yourself of any limitations you may have placed on what's possible. Here, you explore what you desire. Give yourself permission to stretch your imagination.

Who do you want to become? What do you want to achieve? What would you like to do with your life in terms of your relationships with your family, friends and romantic partner? How about your personal growth, finances, career/business or spirituality? Perhaps you want to learn a new skill. Get clear on what your goals are, what's important to you and the direction you want to head.

Step 2: Research the Successful

Who are you inspired by? Research the people who've been successful in achieving the goals you've set for yourself, and study how they became successful. Find out what knowledge and skills are required to reach these goals. Learn from the pitfalls and mistakes they made in their pursuits, so you can save yourself time and energy by not repeating what doesn't work.

Step 3: Evaluate Your Present

Examine your current situation in the various aspects of your life. What's working well and what isn't? What gets you excited? What are your biggest hurdles? What have you done to move forward? What's your number one priority right now?

Step 4: Engineer Your Success Map

You can now engineer your Success Map. This gives you a bird's-eye view of how to get to where you want to go.

Knowing the outcome you desire, you need to plan out all of the actions required in the order in which they need to occur, as well as who will help you perform each of the actions. No man is an island. You will most likely need someone else's help along the way.

Then work out the resources you'll need and fill in the gaps. Establish what to do first and how you can measure your progress. The final part of this step is to leave space for making modifications.

Step 5: Do it

However grand your Success Map, you still need to take action. What you *do* in the present is the key to creating your future, so determine your first step and do it. You can start with a baby step, for sure. If it feels overwhelming, break it down further until you get to a task you feel confident you can do. Remember, Lao simply Tzu said, "The journey of a thousand miles begins with one step."

Step 6: Observe and Assess Your Results

Now it's time to track the actions you've taken and assess your results. It's helpful to have someone keep you accountable, so this is when you would send a photo to your friend or coach to show them you've completed your step. You can also enter it into a log, so you can see your own progress.

This is a time to celebrate! You've done what you set out to do, so feel great about your progress.

Step 7: Modify and Continue

This is the easiest step.

Revisit your Success Map to go over the action steps you've taken and the results you achieved. Then ask yourself these questions:

- Have the results been effective, and what can be improved?
- Are modifications needed to make this a smoother and more efficient process? If so, what are they?
- Are there any issues related to this project, and if so, how can they be solved?
- How inspired do I feel about this project right now?
- What can I do to continue lifting my inspiration?

Then make any necessary modifications to your plan, and continue to cycle through the last three steps in the system.

What are your tips for getting through a difficult time in life?

When faced with a difficult issue or challenge, my suggestion is to get quiet. Go within to gain clarity and receive the answers you need to handle it. This means taking a timeout. It's an important time to check in with yourself in order to reassess the situation and make a decision.

Sometimes you may feel like sleeping and not dealing with it in the moment. If so, allow yourself to sleep on it. You may find you wake up feeling refreshed and better able to tackle what needs to be done.

Writing in a journal also helps, especially when you're not yet ready to talk to someone else about it.

This is a time to be aware of your self-talk. What are you saying to yourself? Remind yourself it's within your power to feel better by changing what you focus on.

Ask for help, and talk to someone you trust about your difficulties, whether it's a coach or a friend. Sometimes you can get stuck in a certain way of thinking and have trouble finding solutions or have an unhelpful attitude about the situation. This person can provide support and encouragement, as well as help guide you towards clarity and a way to move forward.

Another fantastic way to get through a difficult time is to return to gratitude. It can be as simple as taking time to express appreciation and thanks for up to three things that happened that day. This can shift you back to a balanced and centred place where you have a better perspective to deal with your challenges.

How can people be happier in life?

The key to being happier in life is focusing on yourself and tuning into your inner wisdom, as I like to call it.

So often, people seek happiness in all of the wrong places and give their power, the responsibility for their own happiness, to other people. They want someone else to make them happy, be it a friend, lover or family member. On top of that, there's a tendency to focus on what they don't have, instead of appreciating what they do have and enjoying it. Being happier is a simple gift you can give to yourself.

Here are eleven ways to be happier in life. Feel free to pick one that resonates with you and give it a go:

1. Make a list of what you like and appreciate about yourself. Continue adding to that list, and keep it with you always. Read it often.

2. Keep a Gratitude Journal. Each night before bed, write down at least three things you're grateful for, how they make you feel and why you're grateful for them. It could be a stranger's kind gesture, blue skies and sunshine or having your family with you.

3. Move your body. Walk, run, cycle, dance, swim, or do yoga. Get up and move.

Love and Connection

4. Write someone a note of love or thanks.

5. Create physical contact. Hug someone or have a massage.

6. Play! Do something creative and fun you enjoy. Learn a new hobby.

7. Spend time alone. Take yourself on a date. Watch a movie by yourself, go for a long drive or go on a retreat.

8. Invest in your most important relationships. Spend quality time with your closest friends and family, the people who inspire and uplift you.

9. Appreciate what you've experienced. Consider each situation, good and bad, and answer these questions on a piece of paper:

    - What empowering learnings have you gained from this?
    - What's the one biggest lesson you've learnt?
    - What action(s) will you take from here on out, if any?
    - What are you now grateful for?

10. Do a random act of kindness.

11. Learn to meditate. It gives you clarity, better focus and lowers stress.

How can people overcome fear?

You can overcome fear by returning to love. By choosing love. You experience fear when you perceive a threat or danger. Therefore, to overcome fear you can choose to ask yourself different questions, so you can use your powerful imagination in a different way and find the possible positive outcomes, rather than the negative ones.

Instead of asking yourself, *What could go wrong?* ask, *What could go right?* Rather than focusing on what you don't want to happen, place your attention on what you *do* want and *why* you want it. Choose to come from a place of love.

I used to pressure myself to be perfect in everything I did, whether it was forcing my body to get into a certain yoga pose, which is the opposite of its purpose, to striving to get the top score in class, or saying and doing all of the "right" things, so I was a "good" girl and "model" student.

I held so many fears within me, such as fear of failure, rejection and the unknown. These fears often kept me stuck where I was and helped me remain small while keeping me away from what I wanted for myself. Perhaps you could relate.

When you choose to come from a place of love and being of service to others, you'll find the courage to take action, despite your fears. Additionally, when you adopt an attitude of *play* and *discovery*, you'll find your stress and fears melt away, to be replaced by *gratitude* and *excitement*.

You can choose to be thankful for the opportunity and privilege to help someone and a chance to learn something new. Think of the butterflies in your stomach. You get the same feeling whether it's excitement about play or when experiencing nervous energy. It's your choice whether to focus on the nervousness or the excitement.

Uncertainty means possibilities. The unknown means new experiences. New is fun and exciting. Think about it. When children are at play, they're excited and not fearful. I know when I'm enjoying myself, I'm not feeling fear.

How do friends and family affect our lives?

As humans, we all want to bond, and we bond through relationships. That's who we are. It's the way we're built, and it brings meaning to our lives.

Friends and family are some of the most important people you have in your life. From the time you were born, your family starts to shape the way you view situations and people around you. By taking on the beliefs and perspectives of your family, and others, as you grow up, it affects how you see the world. When you have enough self-awareness, you begin to question your beliefs and learn which ones serve you. At that point you can release the ones that don't and create new ones.

You're born into your family. I'm grateful for mine. In so many ways, I've been blessed to have loving parents who've given me so much. They've always been there for me, regardless of what happens. As we mature, my siblings and I have also developed stronger, more intimate relationships. We've learned how to better communicate and appreciate one another.

I like to think of friends as the family you choose for yourself. My good fortune is having more than a handful of kind, compassionate, understanding and accepting friends. They call me to my higher purpose and inspire me through the love they have for life and the challenges I know they've overcome in their own lives. They're amazing people who share in my journey and are amongst the first to receive my good news and celebrate with me. They also hold me accountable and challenge me to grow. They embrace me while I bawl my eyes out and laugh with me till we double over.

Jim Rohn says you're the average of the five people you spend the most time with. Who do you surround yourself with? Do they inspire you? Are they supportive and encouraging towards you? Do they nurture and bring out the best in you?

Go out. Get involved in new activities. Travel. Make new friends. When you continue to grow your friendships, both in quantity and quality, you will expand your circles and increase your chances of having more fulfilling, meaningful relationships in your life.

What's the biggest tip you could give?

It's been said the definition of insanity is doing the same thing over and over again and expecting different results.

Take a new action. It really is that simple. What you've been doing has gotten you this far. If you want a different result, take a different action. Do something new. Break it down. Take the smallest baby steps you can, right now in a new direction. Then take another and another. Before you know it, you'll find yourself in a different place.

 To discover more about how Summer can help you *Elevate Your Life*, simply visit www.elevate-books.com/life

Ria Martinson

Love Your Life

Ria Martinson came to Australia from war-torn Europe with her family, in pursuit of a better life. Her mission was to discover the answers to life's most intriguing questions such as *Who am I?*, *Why am I here?* and *What is my life's purpose?* She's been able to travel the world studying the mind and human potential with some of the world's greatest teachers.

Ria has worked and travelled to India yearly since 1991, visited Mount Shasta in the USA with over two thousand Spiritual Healers during a Wesac Conference in 1997, and trekked in Tibet in 1998 to visit monasteries and other sacred places.

She is a registered Clinical Accredited Mental Health Social Work/Counsellor, Medicare Provider and International Certified Life Coach with an Advanced Diploma in Holistic therapy and a Post-Graduate Certificate in Systemic Family Therapy. Ria has also attained Reiki Level 1 and 2 and is a certified Master Reiki.

Ria Martinson
Love Your Life

What would you like your legacy be?

I would like to be remembered as being an inspiration to my family and everyone I met, and that I inspired them by example to become good and kind people. My best legacy is my contribution to humanity by serving a cause greater than my own. The last and best legacy you can leave is to teach loved ones and others how to live a life of value, become a good person and have love in their life.

Everyone hopes and dreams of the world becoming a better place, so if you work for it in the right way, you can make a huge difference and bring drastic goodness into the world. The good you do doesn't go away. It stays. It's absorbed, accumulated, and adopted long after you're gone. Yes, it's a fact that you will die one day, and it's nothing to be in fear of or sad about.

What would be sad is to not leave any good behind in the world. Whether you live your life well or not, what matters is that you make a positive difference in people's lives, even after you're gone. This happens when you leave a legacy behind that's honoured, respected, valued, and imbibed. It helps them to better their life and spread goodness in the world.

What legacy will you leave behind?

Legacy is inheritance. My gift to my family. Legacy is my act of *gratitude*.

The gift I leave behind becomes the birthright of my people. My gratitude becomes goodness for many. Legacy is powerful, valuable and my best donation to the world. Here are my suggestions for leaving a good legacy:

- Live a life of good values and virtues.

- Develop good habits. Choose the ones that help you be productive, efficient, helpful, and useful.

- Don't
  - lie
  - steal
  - kill
  - cheat
  - hurt people.

- Be healthy, both mentally and physically.

> "We can do no great thing—only small things with great love."
> ~ *Mother Teresa*

What's been your biggest life lesson?

To be true to myself and follow my intuition.

That little voice in the back of your head is there for a reason. Sadly, for many that voice can be self-defeating and quite harsh about life. There are, however, many other occasions where that voice is the megaphone for the heart, telling you what you truly desire and deeply want. Listen to it. Moments of great suffering and sadness make up your core memories. How you cope in these situations can reveal who you really are.

Typically, when you're worried or upset, it's because you've lost perspective. Everything happening in your life seems so big, so important, so do or die, but in the grand picture this single hiccup often means next to nothing. The fight you're having, the job you didn't get, the real or imagined slight, the unexpected need to shift course or the thing you wanted but didn't get, won't matter ten, twenty or thirty years from now. It's hard to see long term when all you know is short term, but unless it's life-threatening, let it go and move on.

Choose to believe this or not, but you're a direct result of your *thought process* and the people you surround yourself with. The beauty of life is that you can make the conscious choice as to what you think, who you spend your time with and what you spend your time doing. I can't speak for you, but I seek people who will always challenge, encourage and push me to grow.

Judgment and negative energy are a reflection of the giver, not the receiver. People who spend a lot of time judging others generally spend little time working on themselves. When you put your energy into your own life and choices, you stop focusing on everyone else. The road to truly believing in yourself is paved with knowing and accepting yourself, flaws and all. Walking that journey also makes you much more compassionate and aware that others may also be travelling down a path you can't see.

People often don't appreciate what they have until it's gone. That includes health, family and friends, their job and the money they have, or think they will have in the future.

When you're young, it seems your parents will always be there, but they won't. You think you have plenty of time to get back in touch with your old friends or spend time with new ones, but you don't. You have the money to spend, or you think you'll have it next month, but you might not. Nothing in life is guaranteed to be there tomorrow, including those you love.

One of the major regrets people have is taking life too seriously. Bad situations are bound to happen, sure, but they're probably not as bad as you make them out to be in your head. And isn't life way more fun if you're chuckling along with it?

Authentically confident people are inspiring. When you truly believe in yourself, you hold the power of influence. Others will want to aid your efforts. This is especially important if you're growing a business or embarking on any endeavour that requires support. This is a hard life lesson to learn, but it may be the most important of all: life can change in an instant, so make sure you appreciate what you have, while you still have it.

> "Life is what happens while you're busy making other plans."
> *~ John Lennon*

What does love mean to you?

Love is more than a feeling. It's a choice.

That burst of initial exhilaration, pulse-quickening love and passion doesn't last long, but that doesn't mean long-lasting love isn't possible. Love isn't just a feeling, it's a choice you make every day. You have to choose to let annoyances pass and forgive. Be kind, respectful, supportive and faithful. Relationships take work. Sometimes it's easy, and sometimes it's incredibly difficult, but it's up to you to choose how you want to act, think and speak in a relationship.

Ria Martinson

Trust **L**istening
Romance **O**vercoming
Understanding **V**aluable
Excitement **E**verything

If you were speaking to your younger self, what advice would you give?

There are so many lessons I wish I'd learned while I was young enough to appreciate and apply them. Here's the advice I would give.

Love yourself first.

The thing with wisdom, and often with life lessons in general, is that they're learned in retrospect, long after you needed them. The good news is that other people can benefit from your experiences and the lessons you've learned. You don't need everyone to agree with you, or even like you. It's human nature to want to belong and to be liked, respected and valued, but not at the expense of your integrity and happiness. Other people can't give you the validation you seek. That has to come from within. Speak up, stick to your guns, and assert yourself when you need to, demand respect and stay true to your values.

Even if you feel hatred, keep it to yourself. Don't hurt other people for any reason.

Love Your Life

- Find your passion and live it.
- Take action.
- Don't ever give up on love.
- Nobody else controls you.
- Make time to cry.
- Travel while you're young and able. Don't worry about the money. Just make it work. Experience is far more valuable than money will ever be.
- Don't compare yourself to others, or you'll never be happy with your life. The grass is always greener.
- If you're embarrassed to be dating someone, you shouldn't be dating them.
- Do one thing each day that's just for you.
- Don't be a cheapskate.
- Forgive.
- Most of the time, everything will work itself out.
- Live life with gratitude.
- Learn to adapt.
- Take time to mourn what you've lost.

Far too many people are good at vocalising the life they want but not near as good at putting a plan into action to get there. It's not enough to dream out loud or inside of your head. You must absolutely put yourself out there and leap into action.

You can relate to the struggles and battles that life brings, but that doesn't mean you have to roll over and take it. It's tough, sure, but anything that's worthwhile is. It really comes down to a simple choice: struggle for fulfilment now or wish you had during your final moments. The truth is, hard work and determination will get you through the most difficult times in your life. Struggles teach you to be resourceful and find a way out of a difficult situation.

As the song says, "Everybody hurts...sometimes." Social norms mandate that you keep these feelings to yourself. If you must, share your pain only with those closest to you. In addition to experiencing joy, laughter, exhilaration, and awe, you will experience sadness, anger, shame, confusion, and guilt.

You could benefit from taking a page out of Buddhist traditions, which includes *dukkha*, or suffering, as a central concept. The Buddhist approach acknowledges that, by its very nature, life is difficult, flawed and imperfect. *Dukkha* is a natural part of life and can only be eradicated in a lifelong journey towards enlightenment.

Modern science also recognizes that negative emotions are a necessary part of life, and a component of its role is to grab your attention and alert you of potential dangers. Again, just like you, everybody hurts sometimes, even the people who seem the most outgoing, optimistic, and fun.

Only you can decide. The solitary obstacle standing in your way of happiness is you. No one else is allowed to set up your limits but you. Nor should there be. No matter what kind of problems you're dealing with, how old you are or where you live, you deserve to be happy. It's as simple as that. It's time to face the fact that you're in control of your future and finally do something about it.

Everyone around you will try to dictate what you are or who you should be, but don't you let them. No one needs to validate your worth besides you, and you'll someday deeply regret it if you spend your life pleasing the world around you. Don't worry about pleasing your parents, friends, or bosses. You need to worry about number one, first and foremost. Always.

What do you think is your life's purpose?

To be kind to all I meet.

How would you like to be remembered?

With love.

I want people to remember me as someone who was easy to talk to, a great friend and a good listener. As someone who was caring, kind and generous.

I hope to be remembered as someone who:

- extended love to others
- cared deeply about the environment, people and animals
- was an extremely loving mother and grandmother
- inspired others to live a life they love
- appreciated the simple things in life
- valued time with family and friends
- enjoyed nature and walking
- enjoyed exercise and valued health and happiness

- respected others' opinions
- set goals and was determined to keep growing, changing and learning
- was not externally or materialistically minded
- was compassionate
- had a faith that was important to her
- was interested in spirituality
- always saw the best in everyone
- was patient
- never gave up, no matter what

> Live the way you want to be remembered.

Why is mindset important?

I firmly believe who you are on a day-to-day basis comes from your *mindset*. It's the view you have of your qualities and characteristics. Where they come from and whether they can change. The following two mindsets represent the extreme ends of the spectrum.

- *Fixed mindset*

    This mindset comes from the belief that your qualities are carved in stone. Who you are is who you are, period. Characteristics such as intelligence, personality, and creativity are fixed traits, rather than something that can be developed and changed.

    Having a fixed mindset creates an urgency to prove yourself over and over. Criticism is seen as an attack on your character and to be avoided.

- *Growth mindset*

    This comes from the belief that your basic qualities can be cultivated through effort. People differ greatly in aptitude, talents, interests, or temperaments, but everyone can change and grow through application and experience. Having a growth mindset encourages learning and effort. If you truly believe you can improve, you will be much more driven to learn and practice.

    Criticism is seen as valuable feedback and openly embraced. The hallmark of the growth mindset is the passion for sticking with it, *especially* when life isn't going well.

    Mindset isn't just important for learning new skills. It can affect the way that you think about what happens to you. For example, a growth mindset can help you recover from illness, because you believe you can do something about it. A good mindset can help you achieve in sport or at work and can also help you grow and develop in relationships. Cultivating a growth mindset could be the single most important attribute you can ever develop to help you achieve success.

What do you think people's biggest life issues are?

Self-esteem and believing in themselves.

The biggest of all challenges is something called *procrastination*, which everyone's experienced and are yet not yet able to give up. Procrastination has become so compulsive, people are slaves to it.

What's the reason? Why do you postpone and not make the most of the time you have? The main reason is that most people, and I'm including myself, aren't responsible enough, daring enough, crazy enough and bold enough to take a stand for what they want of themselves and what they want their life to be.

What do you want to achieve? You may be confused with so many questions from all over the universe. They aren't difficult. They're already answered, and you can make them vanish with a few decisions. The effect these questions have is that you tend to be tired of answering them in a million ways. They tend to distract and confuse you all throughout your career and while you're studying. These questions waste your time thinking about them. As a result, you lose interest in studies and other current, important issues.

The only way out of the maze is to find your passion. Ha! Look how easily I said that. I know it's difficult, and I'm sailing in the same boat, but I've heard people say, "Whatever you have right now is important, so work on that with dedication, and maybe you will find your passion in the path."

Again, I'm working on it as well, but my personal belief is this: the best way to find your passion is *self-belief*. With this in mind, have faith in yourself and move forward on your path.

What's the best way to help people with procrastination?

You know what you want to do and should do, but you still end up spending hours upon hours doing easier work or escaping via TV, blogs or music. Now, there's nothing wrong with a little escape from time to time, but if you procrastinate too much, you won't get the most important tasks done. You will also send yourself into negative spirals where your self-esteem plummets, and you spend your days in a vague, negative funk.

So what can you do? Here are seven timeless tips to help you stop procrastinating and start living your life more fully.

1. Stop thinking. Start doing.

> "To think too long about doing a thing
> often becomes its undoing."
> *~ Eva Young*

A bit of planning can certainly help you to achieve what you want. A lot of planning and thinking tends to have the opposite effect. You think and think and try to come up with *the perfect plan* where you don't have to make mistakes, will never be rejected, and there will be no pain or difficulties. Such a thing, of course, doesn't exist. But as long as you work on that plan, you can protect yourself.

2. Don't blow a task out of proportion.

> "If you want to make an easy job seem mighty hard, just keep putting off doing it."
> *~ Olin Miller*

> "Putting off an easy thing makes it hard. Putting off a hard thing makes it impossible."
> ~ *George Claude Lorimer*

By over-thinking and procrastinating, you're not only trying to protect yourself from pain, you also make mountains out of molehills. The quotes above are so true, it isn't even funny. The more hours and days you put something off, the worse it grows in your mind, because you're dwelling on it, and so it expands. Since you're putting it off, you're also probably thinking about it in a negative way. This makes a little problem a big Godzilla, a horrible beast that's threatening to ruin your life. So plan a little, and then take action.

Often you don't even have to plan. You've been there before, and you know what needs to be done. So stop thinking and *just do it*, no matter how you feel and what you think. What you're feeling right can change as quickly as the weather, so it's not the perfect guidance system, and you don't have to obey what it says. It's not chains made of iron. You can just do what you know is right, anyway.

3. Just take the first step.

> "You don't have to see the whole staircase, just take the first step."
> ~ *Martin Luther King, Jr.*

When you start to look too far into the future, any task or project can seem close to impossible, so you shut down, become overwhelmed and start surfing the internet aimlessly instead. That's one of the reasons why it's good to plan for the future but then shift your focus back to today and the present moment.

Then focus daily on taking the first step. That's all you need to do. By taking the first step you change your mental state from resistant to, *Hey, I'm doing this. Cool!* You put yourself in a state where you become more positive and open. You may not be enthusiastic about taking the second step, but you at least accept it. Then you can take the next step, and the one after that.

The thing is, you can't see the whole staircase anyway, and it will shift and reveal itself along the way. That's why the best of plans tend to fall apart at least a bit as you start to put it into action. You discover your map of reality doesn't look like reality.

4. Start with the hardest task of your day.

> "Do the hard jobs first. The easy jobs will take care of themselves."
> *~ Dale Carnegie*

Maybe you have an important call to make you fear might be uncomfortable. Maybe you know you've gotten behind on answering your emails and have a big pile to dig into. Maybe you have the last five pages of your paper to finish.

Whatever it may be, get it out of your way first.

If you start your day like this, you'll feel relieved, relaxed and good about yourself. Then the rest of the day, and your to-do list, tend to feel a lot lighter and easier to move through. It's amazing what a difference this one action makes.

5. Just make a decision. Any decision.

> "In a moment of decision, the best thing you can do is the right thing to do, the next best thing is the wrong thing, and the worst thing you can do is nothing."
> ~ Theodore Roosevelt

You feel bad when you sit on your hands and don't take action, because it's unnatural. *The natural thing is to be a decisive human and take action.*

When you procrastinate, you want to take action that's in alignment with your thoughts but don't. Then you become conflicted within.

When you procrastinate, you lower your self-esteem and send signals back to your brain that you're, well, kind of a lame and indecisive person. What you do always sends signals back about who you are. Sure, doing affirmations where you tell yourself you're confident can help, but taking confident actions over and over again is what really builds your self-confidence and a good self-image, so you can be a confident person.

6. Face your fear.

> "Procrastination is the fear of success. People procrastinate because they are afraid of the success that they know will result if they move ahead now. Because success is heavy, carries a responsibility with it, it is much easier to procrastinate and live on the 'someday I'll' philosophy."
> ~ Denis Whitley

I think this is true. It's easier to live on that *someday*... thought and much harder to just take action and risk looking like a fool. To make mistakes, stumble, not avoid that pain and take responsibility for your own life.

The easier choice can come with a sense of comfort and a certain level of success, but along with it there will be pangs of regret for all you never dared go for and a vague sense of being unfulfilled. You wonder about what would have happened if you'd taken more action and more chances. You may not know what the harder choice gives you, but it will sure make your feel more alive.

7. Finish it.

> "Nothing is as fatiguing as the eternal hanging on of an uncompleted task."
> ~ William James

> "Much of the stress that people feel doesn't come from having too much to do. It comes from not finishing what they started."
> ~ David Allen

Not taking the first step towards accomplishment can make you feel bad. But not finishing what you've started can also leave you in a sort of negative funk. You feel fatigued or stressed, and sometimes you don't even know why. It's like someone sapped your inner power.

If that's the case, go over tasks and projects in which you're currently involved. Is there something you know you want to finish but haven't yet? Try to get that out of the way as soon as you can, and you'll start to feel a whole lot better. Just be careful. Don't think you have to finish everything you started. If a book is unsatisfying, read something else. But using this as an excuse to quit a task that feels hard or unfamiliar isn't a good idea, either. Figure out what's important, and not important, to complete.

What courses have you taken that enabled you to get started or build your business?

I am a registered Clinical Accredited Mental Health Social Work/Counsellor, Medicare Provider, and an International Certified Life Coach with an Advanced Diploma in Holistic therapy.

I have a post-graduate Certificate in Systemic Family Therapy, and with this I also attained my Reiki Level 1 and 2 and am a certified Reiki Master.

I have worked on a higher spiritual level with the masters and am a certified Melchezidek trainer.

I've also had many personal experiences of creating abundance and parallel life forms. My belief is that there are many life forms in the universe, and this journey on Earth is to become *one* with all. *I am that I am.*

In your experience, what's the biggest tip you could give to people?

Compare yourself to yourself instead of comparing yourself to others. See how much you've grown, what you've achieved and what progress you've made towards your goals. This habit has the benefit of creating gratitude, appreciation and kindness towards yourself as you observe how far you've come, the obstacles you've overcome and the good stuff you've done. You feel good about yourself without having to think less of other people.

Remember that you can't win if you keep comparing yourself to others. Just consciously realizing this can be helpful. No matter what you do, you can find someone else in the world who has more than you or is better than you at something.

Focus on the positive in yourself and in the people around you. Appreciate what's positive in yourself and others. This way you become more okay with yourself and the people in your world, instead of ranking them, and yourself, and creating differences in your mind.

Be kind. In my experience, the way you behave and think towards others seems to have a big, big effect on how you behave towards and think about yourself. Judge and criticize people, and you tend to judge and criticize yourself more, often almost automatically. Be kinder to others and help them, and you tend to be kinder and more helpful to yourself.

What is the one message you wish to share with the world?

Be kind to yourself, and take time to smell the roses.

Ria Martinson

 To discover more about how Ria can help you *Elevate Your Life*, simply visit

www.elevate-books.com/life

Elinor Salmon
Reawakening Your Identity

Since she was a small child, Elinor Salmon has been a keen participant in any activity that piqued her interest, whether it was dancing, swimming, playing the saxophone or ice skating. She's always believed in pursuing your dreams, helping others and providing opportunities to those who may not have them. At the age of sixteen she shaved her head for cancer.

In 2010 Elinor received the Gold Duke of Edinburgh award and delivered the acceptance speech at Government House to Governor Maree Bashieer of NSW. She was also awarded the Pittwater Council youth volunteer of the year award in 2010.

Elinor has skated and danced competitively and in shows since the age of three. She's still pursuing her love of ice skating and is expanding her abilities into life coaching and public speaking.

Elinor Salmon

Reawakening Your Identity

What does identity mean to you?

The dictionary definition of identity is *a set of characteristics by which a person or thing is definitively recognisable.*

Until recently, I had identified myself by my ice skating and never thought about how I let this significant part of my life become me. My skating was *what* I did for a job not *who* I was.

Identity is the essence of what you are and how you choose to express it. People are shape shifters, so whatever medium they connect with will be how they express themselves for a period of time before moving on to the next.

I believe this is why only physical characteristics and occupation are used to describe people. Trying to illustrate someone's soul identity in one word is impossible.

Do you think your parents helped shape your identity?

I was never one to completely excel in school, but I gave it a shot. I did excel in my extracurricular activities and would throw myself into them. I was fortunate to have parents who didn't force me into an activity but instead let me follow my own interests.

When I was going through school I was always asked why I wasn't going out to someone's party or to a particular event lots of people were invited to. My response was always the same. "Sorry. I would love to, but I have skating in the morning" or "Sorry, I have a carnival that weekend."

Reawakening Your Identity

Because of this, it was easier for people not to invite me. There were times I felt alone and disconnected from my peers, but looking back now I realise these were boundaries I'd set for myself. It gave me perspective as to what was important to me. But then somewhere along the way I suppressed my needs and became so focused on helping and doing for others that I stopped doing what I really loved.

If I ever complained about not going to an event, my parents were quick to remind me I could go, but it would mean taking time from one of my activities. I learned to keep my mouth shut and reminded myself that I wanted to participate in dance, skating, saxophone and swimming. My mum and dad didn't particularly enjoy getting up early and driving me everywhere, and I'm sure they would have happily spent the money somewhere else, but they were always there to support me in every way. If I complained they would remind me with the words, "You don't have to."

My parents thought it was important for me to set my own standards and boundaries to achieve what I wanted. I believe this is what's missing in the education of the younger generation.

By setting my own boundaries when I was younger, I never felt the need to try drugs or alcohol. I already had a number of activities that elevated me and allowed me to express myself in many positive ways. I wasn't going to do something that wouldn't give me the same fulfilment as what I was already doing.

Why do you think teens push their boundaries in negative ways?

There's a traditional system that implies what's right and what's wrong, yet not every child will work to that system, and quite a large percentage will see it as a challenge to break the rules as a form of expression.

Elinor Salmon

I believe it's important to understand that most adolescents turn to drugs and alcohol because they're given a set of boundaries that don't fulfil their own values. If they don't succeed in the traditional system, they're seen as a failure. They're told they *can't* do something or they *failed* that exam, so they push or break these boundaries as a form of expression and belonging. If this continues for a period of time of course they're going to take some kind of action, even if it's a negative one, just to get noticed.

In a society of media influence and social combat, identity has become one of the hardest ideals to strive for and be proud of. People fail to believe in themselves so much, they create multiple identities to hide their true selves.

So many people feel they'll never be accepted or have the perfect life, so they hide behind a façade of a happy face, expensive restaurants, parties and amazing travel destinations to fake it for a while. This portrayal of the "perfect" life is shown as a movie reel on social media and provides the adoration missing from their real life.

What makes this infinite portal more special than the amazing life they've been given? In a generation of (I) pads, (I) phones and social MEdia, people have become so self obsessed with competition for the life they think they should have, they don't appreciate the one they do.

The younger generation has been conditioned to be disempowered before they've had the chance to live. I think there are opportunities being missed for the younger generations to make a change to be remembered by, instead of getting the attention by harming themselves or taking it too far. I want to make clear that I don't mean to undermine parents, because they're doing the best they can within the system. Yet I think it's very important to start really connecting with children to find out what they want to achieve and not disregard any creative ideas they have. Let them live to their higher values.

When you were growing up, did you have identity issues?

If I review my entire childhood and teenage years, I can say I never had an issue with who I was or what I looked like. I did activities I enjoyed, I ate whatever I wanted, and I didn't worry about how much I weighed or what I had to do to please anyone. I loved exploring new ideas, expanding my creative list and dabbling in any creative or sporting activity.

I never really fit in at school and was always little bit of a drifter. I didn't just have one set of friends I hung out with, but I connected well with people older than I was, and I guess that made me a little weird. However, that never stopped me from doing it.

During high school there was an opportunity for me to explore and learn new skills. I started the Duke of Edinburgh Bronze Award in year 9 and continued through to completion of my Gold Award in 2010. This gave me a whole new opportunity to do orienteering, which I hadn't done before, combined with hiking and camping, which had never been high on my list, but I really enjoyed them.

Duke of Ed supplied a solid foundation to expand my horizons and push myself to new heights. I forged friendships with peers and teachers and begin to realise that anything I set my mind to was truly possible. I was able to go back and help the younger teens come through their own awards and assist them in their development along their journey. This gave me such a sense of fulfilment that I just wanted to keep doing it.

At that time, I had a session with my careers advisor, and he asked what I wanted to do when I finished school. My initial response was, "Save the world." He laughed and said," I love it, but how about you break it down?"

I never had a proper idea of what career I wanted, but superhuman being sounded pretty good to me.

This spurred me on to a huge amount of fundraising for all different causes. If I couldn't save the whole world, then at least I could make a positive impact in some way. Helping people really lights me up, and at least knowing I was able to make a small, but significant, difference in someone's life was enough for me.

My favourite fundraiser came around in 2009 for the World's Greatest Shave, which raised money for Leukaemia. Within a week I decided to shave my head and do all of the fundraising to have it ready for the official date. $5000.00 and a missing ponytail later, I was a walking shoe brush of liberation. I'd never felt anything like it. Freedom, empowerment and liberation enveloped me for weeks.

While I was attending State Music Camp, there was a boy named Jack who asked me why I shaved my head. I told him, and all he said was, "Thank you. You saved my life. I was cleared from my leukaemia only three weeks ago." This is a moment in time I will always cherish, because I knew I'd been a part of something that had made a profound difference in someone's life.

I was complete with who I was.

Was there a point when you started having identity issues?

When I began my professional career in ice skating, I was faced with a realisation about my body image and how I had to fit a mould. I saw it as a challenge and a new chapter I hadn't really explored before. What's unfortunate is that it wound up consuming me, and I took it too far.

As I now reflect on that time, I realize it was the beginning of my loss of identity.

I was bigger than the other girls, weighing 65kgs and 5ft7 in height, which is not overweight but was still "too big". These girls were all

Reawakening Your Identity

fulltime showgirls or had just finished competition, and they were at their physical peak. They knew how their bodies worked and what they needed to do to before the opening of the show came around.

This was entirely new to me. Nobody told me I was required to weigh a certain amount, do my own makeup, wear particular hairstyles and fix my costumes for minor repairs. It's unfortunate I found out the hard way when I was made an example of in front of the entire cast. I was pointed out by the producer who said, "Girls, this is what I don't want you to look like." Pretty scary for anyone.

I was weighed every day and fined out of my pay cheque if I didn't lose the weight, so I did pretty much what any person would have done without any decent nutritional understanding: I cut my food back more and more and trained harder and harder at the gym. I also did a show every night. Sometimes two.

From my first weigh-in at 65kg, within five months I dropped to 58kg. I was *so* proud of myself. When I noticed I could get away with not eating, or eating the smallest amount possible, there was that little dark voice in my head that told me, *If you've already done this much, why can't you do more*? In October 2012 was when I really began my journey into the darker world of body image. I became obsessed. I would swim 1.5km a day or spend at least an hour in the gym, and then I'd do the show in the evenings. I'd never eat past 6pm and generally ate nothing more than maybe some salad or an apple for dinner.

For one year I never let myself weigh more than 54.6kg. As I continued further down the rabbit hole of twisted identity and body image, the little voice in my head got louder. It said, *What would happen if you went further?* So I did.

When I finally came home in Jan 2014, I weighed in at what I realise now was a shocking 42.4kg. In eighteen months I'd lost 20kg and stayed there for a period of time. The scariest part is that I was proud of myself. I thought I'd finally figured out the secret to being a stunning ice skater. The skinnier you are, the more elegant you look on the ice. We do, after all, sell an image.

Did you realise you had lost your identity?

Not at all. I just knew I was unhappy, yet I accepted that sometimes that's just the way it is. While working all over the world, performing in different countries with different people for three years and only coming home for short periods of time, I thought I had life figured out.

I knew which company I was going to be working for and where I was going to be a year in advance. I had the support of my family and a man who was both my skating partner and boyfriend. I loved my job, the travel, the people I got to work with and the great experiences. Yet for a number of months there was a void that couldn't be filled no matter how much space my boyfriend gave me or how good I felt about my job. There was something I craved, but I couldn't figure it out. For months I felt like my entire world was spinning out of control, and I was just along for the ride. I convinced myself it was all in my head and to stop being dramatic.

I aimed so high to be the perfect girlfriend and skating partner, that I lost sight of me. What I really loved to do had been pushed aside to allow more time to devote to being this unattainable image I'd conjured inside of my head. Yet still I tried.

I was successful, though I felt like an empty shell that if pushed too hard would shatter into a million pieces. I had made my relationship "perfect" but only if everything was well organized.

Through confirmation from others, I believed I'd created a perfect relationship with my boyfriend. In retrospect, we had. We never fought and came to a compromise on every issue. We liked spending time together and took interest in whatever new activity the other was doing. We worked, trained and lived together.

Yet I look back now and have to ask what my identity was. I shifted and changed so much to fit the mould that I wouldn't have been able to tell anyone what my soul identity was. I thought my skating made me who I was, and without it I was nothing.

What made you realise you're allowed to be happy in life?

A comment from my friend Roman hit me like a truck. I thought I'd been doing a wonderful job of wearing my mask of happiness, until he turned to me in the middle of a show and asked, "Where's your smile?" I gave him my best showgirl smile and a wink. He looked at me with complete compassion and said, "That's beautiful, but your eyes are dead. Are you sure you're okay? I don't know what's going on, but you're allowed to be happy. You know that, right?"

From that moment, I knew I couldn't keep this façade going anymore. I needed to stop being scared of what would happen without my skating and boyfriend in the picture and just be happy and free to reconnect with me. Roman gave me the permission I didn't realize I'd been waiting for, and I began doing everything just for me. Now, some of what I did was fairly extreme. I will admit it all happened in rapid succession.

- I went travelling by myself for two weeks.
- I broke up with my boyfriend, which meant giving up a year of work.
- I stopped skating for a while and funnelled large amounts of savings into my education.
- I got a tattoo.

I'm not saying everyone needs to go to this extreme, but you need to give yourself permission to be happy and live the life you deserve.

I look back on my life and realise that for everyone on the outside, my decisions were a huge surprise, especially for my boyfriend. He had the rug ripped out from underneath him. His life changed just as much as mine did, and I hope in the future we can both appreciate what we had to learn from each other.

I think having these major changes and rapid shifts has been easier than trying to implement them all slowly.

How did you begin to reconnect with your Identity?

My friend, Lee, recently asked me, "Who are you?" and went on to say I wasn't allowed to answer with what I did, because that wasn't who I was.

I spent a full day trying to find the words to answer the question. At first, I think I managed to use only two words to describe me: unique and individual. But these words apply to everyone.

Once I figured out it was an exercise to discover who *I am*, the words started flowing.

I ended up answering not with the *who* but more the *I am*, which gave me room for more expansion about what made me unique.

Give it a go. Take a piece of paper and write I AM in the middle of the page, so you can add to it when you think of what comprises what you are. Give yourself permission. You deserve to acknowledge the amazing being you are. There's nothing wrong with being unique. It's one-hundred percent natural.

Reawakening Your Identity

This exercise may be a challenge, especially if you've suppressed what makes up your identity and don't want to acknowledge how wonderful you truly are.

It was an empowering moment for me when I realised that once I re-empowered myself, my identity began to shine through, and I wasn't scared of what I could achieve.

What's one of the biggest discoveries you've come to terms with?

One of the biggest lessons I've learnt in the short amount of time I've been on this wonderful planet is that everyone deserves to live the life that gives them the most fulfilment, without fear of judgment from others. Everyone should have the confidence to be who they are without worrying about not being enough.

Society has conditioned everyone to strive for standards so high they're unattainable, yet they're seen as normal. People strive for the perfect body, job and life. Why can't everyone just enjoy what they have and live how they want?

Looking back on my own experience, I can say it's a wonderful feeling to pull back a veil and see that what I needed and yearned for was just to be comfortable in my own skin and think, *I am enough.*.

After struggling with body image for a number of years, I look back at photos and wonder why I thought I was unattractive. I'd let my perception of ice skating and performing define *who* I was. It was only *what* I did, but I'd let it become my identity.

I look at younger teens now through a completely different filter. All I want is for them to realise what I'm realising now, which is how amazing they are.

Elinor Salmon

What advice would you give your younger self?

Don't ever think anything you've done will define you for your entire life. It will be a beautiful chapter you can always look back on and appreciate for the lessons you've learnt.

No matter what people think of you, continue in the direction of your dreams. The challenges of staying on that path will be hard, but it will be worth it. If you want to change your mind at any point, that's okay. You don't need worry about anyone else. Don't be afraid to do what you love and succeed at it.

Society will shift and change, and you will lose some of your friends. But if you stay true to yourself, you will have the best and most supportive network you could ask for.

Don't let the opportunities you desire pass you by, because you were afraid to hurt someone's feelings. Take the plunge that most terrifies you, and don't to be afraid to fail. You have the resources to push yourself in the right direction.

You will always be enough. There's nothing more you need to offer. Aiming to overachieve or taking on too many responsibilities will only give you chaos that seems uncontrollable, when all you need to do is ask for a little help, say no when enough is enough and follow your heart.

What's the one message you want to share with the world?

Once you begin to take back your own identity and stop living to others' expectations, you can be truly happy. If you're sharing your life with someone special, then it should be because you help to enhance each other's happiness.

Reawakening Your Identity

Once you have happiness within yourself, you can live authentically. When you live entirely with your heart, there's nothing that can stop you from achieving what you desire most.

Why do people believe they can't change?

There's only a minority of people who would say change is easy, and you shouldn't be afraid. A majority will say that if you change too much, you'll throw off the balance you created. But have we as a society really created this balance? Looking at people living outside of the so-called norm, you may think, *I wish I could have such a simple life.*

Why can't you? Because you've been conditioned from a young age to believe:

- you aren't allowed to do what you want
- it's wrong to do what you want
- you need to stop drawing attention to yourself
- you need to fit in with the others
- you need to go out and get a decent-paying job

These examples resonate on some level and define smaller events that have changed the way you perceive the life you live.

You fit in, because it's what everyone else is doing. You get a job you don't totally enjoy, because what you would love to do is just a dream and "silly". You may think getting a different haircut or going on a diet is a radical change, but why can't they just be ways to enhance your lifestyle in a positive way? And often when you make these changes, you get comments, judgment and gossip from others to immediately revert back to what you were before.

Elinor Salmon

No wonder people feel like change is impossible!

Why do you think people become overwhelmed in finding their identity?

> "Waking up to who you are requires letting go of who you imagined yourself to be."
> ~ *Alan Watts*

Finding yourself after you've suppressed who you are for so long is an overwhelming process. I can relate. One of my most amazing discoveries is that when you go on a journey of enlightenment, you need to realise you're already enlightened. What you're really on a journey for is wholeness.

Once you begin the process of taking your masks off, you become truly vulnerable and allow your pure self to shine through. You've reached enlightenment and can begin your soul journey of wholeness.

When I started letting go of everything I thought made me who I was, it was terrifying. I held on for a little longer, so I didn't feel like I'd just thrown everything away, but that's what needed to happen.

It's so easy to revert back to what you've been portraying for so long. Changing and implementing new values and ideas is confronting. You continue to wonder what people think and hope that you will hold onto the same friends and support network. I think what you need to realize is that once you begin to allow yourself to flourish, everything will shift.

Does technology help or hinder?

Everyone uses technology, and it's helped society in reconnecting with people all over the world at the click of a button. You can't deny the positives, but just like with every positive, there are negatives. I think people need to pay attention and recognise when technology overtakes reality.

Why are young men and women being brainwashed with images of beautiful people who've been airbrushed to look a certain way, when the aim should be achieve a healthier version of themselves? Why are only depressing acts displayed on the news, when there's so much happiness and peace out there? No wonder everyone tries to escape their lives through mobile phones, music, Instagram, Facebook, and Twitter. They're bored trying to attain the unattainable and live a real life, so they seek validation in an idealistic world. It becomes more important than travelling or having a romantic dinner no one else knows about, because if there's no proof, it didn't happen.

Yet by living this way, you miss the beautiful moments that shape your life.

What's one of the best experiences you've ever had?

Travelling by myself, without a doubt, is one of the best experiences I've ever had. Getting lost in different cities of countries where I couldn't speak the language, while creating memories just for me. Opening up and doing what I really loved without worrying if I was making someone else bored, because it wasn't what they wanted to do. I realised I loved my own company, and I was comfortable with it. I didn't have an agenda to fill or a need to meet someone else's expectations. All I did was fulfil my own dreams and desires.

During this time is when I realized my ice skating didn't define me. I loved my partner, yet what we shared as a couple I'd let characterise me as an individual.

What can someone do to regain their identity?

Listen to yourself, do what you love and don't think about other people's judgements or comments. Your intuition is so much stronger than you think, and by doing what you love, you begin to live your desires. Reawakening and realising what you truly are is a scary process, but I think it's when you begin to empower yourself again and live authentically that you reconnect with your soul identity.

I'm not saying by any stretch of the imagination that it will be a simple process, but the change can be easy if you listen to your heart's desire and live from there instead of your head, so you can unleash your identity and potential.

When I began this process, I discovered my attitude shifted about a lot of situations, especially characteristics I thought had been faults and imperfections. They've turned into resources I could draw upon.

I'm so excited about everything the future holds, and I can't wait to share it with everyone I encounter. I guess after the life experience I've had and now going through the process of regaining my identity, I can sum it up in one line: *What you see is what you get.*

What would you like to do in life?

Help younger generations on their own journey of identity and empowerment and get them to understand the life they've been given has so much more meaning than they've been conditioned to believe. They have every right to dream and aspire to be something bigger and achieve goals above and beyond the constrictions of society.

I had this idea I wouldn't be able to help anyone after being told quite a few times over, "We'd trust someone older" or "We're looking for someone with more experience". I began to think that until I got older, I wouldn't be able to help anyone. Yet I realised that if I kept waiting, my dreams would stall, and if I kept redefining what old enough was, I'd be dead. By using my age in a positive manner, it allows me to connect to the younger generation, because I've just come from where they are. I'm still exploring and learning about owning my identity.

> "You read and write and sing and experience, hoping that one day those things will build the character you admire to live as. You love and lose and bleed, best you can, to the extreme, hoping that one day the world will read you like the poem you want to be."
> ~ *Charlotte Eriksson*

 To discover more about how Elinor can help you *Elevate Your Life*, simply visit www.elevate-books.com/life

Ilona Vass

Dancing with the Dragons

Ilona Vass is the founder and owner of Dancing with the Dragons, which gives her the opportunity to accompany and assist people to feel confident when handling difficult and challenging situations and equip them on their journey to a better life. She's passionate about intercultural communication, group dynamics and the power of mindset and specializes in helping people achieve results by working with instant, practical applications.

Due to her wealth of business experience in sales and general management from her previous career in aviation, Ilona has a highly enthusiastic and down-to-earth approach with her clients in communication and leadership trainings, personal coaching and intercultural advice. Ilona is a true cosmopolitan, having lived in Austria, China and Australia and is fluent in German, English and Mandarin.

Ilona Vass

Dancing with the Dragons

Her motto is, "We all get presented with lemons in life. Let's make lemonade!"

What's your biggest life lesson?

I'm grateful I learnt my life lesson early on. It's the belief that there's always light again after a dark or tough period, and after a *down* there will always be an *up* again. Trusting in this life cycle means having the power to live in positivity and flexibility. This belief has allowed me to push through a few challenging times in life. It's given me the ability to cultivate unknown strengths, as well as the desire to develop myself as a human being. I see this as an ongoing journey. In all of my relationships with clients, friends and family, I encourage them to have the same trust.

If you were speaking to your younger self, what advice would you give?

I would say, "It's not necessary to always try to please others and put yourself second."

In the past I've given in on too many demands and over-adapted to unhealthy situations. This only stressed me out and put unnecessary pressure on myself.

Being there for others is still a core value for me, but it's developed a different connotation I wish I could have understood earlier. Nowadays it means I can only assist others when I'm centred and look after myself as well. This by no means implies it's good to be self-centred or to roll over other human beings. It means having equality.

I would also tell my younger self to start with self-development and healthy mental practices much earlier and to focus not only on professional skills training, but equally on soft skills training.

What's the worst thing that's ever happened to you, and how did you overcome it?

It was definitely an accumulation of incidences in 2010 when my father, who I was close with, passed away. Then a couple of weeks later my ex-partner, the father of my son, ended our relationship abruptly. As a result, I was driven into a court case that lasted a couple of years and ended in financial disaster. Not being in my home country of Austria with my family made me feel lonely at that time, despite having many wonderful friends here.

At that time I felt the universe was pulling the carpet from under my feet, and I was in freefall. My self-esteem was at rock bottom. I couldn't grieve for my losses in a healthy way, and my world collapsed. My whole self switched into a kind of survival mode, and I developed a strength I never knew I had.

What got me through and out of this painful and stressful period was a consistent pursuit of learning new techniques to manage mindset, while undergoing various qualifications. All of these efforts helped me, bit by bit, to come back to myself. But it was a different self. An evolved self. A self who more and more followed a passion to offer other human beings helpful tools and options so they'd never give up, believe in the light at the end of a tunnel and become content and successful.

Have you had any aha moments that changed everything for you?

Absolutely. An important one was when I got to know the Process Communication Model® (PCM) developed by Dr Taibi Kahler. This communication tool is different from others, as it's based on psychological insights. I got so fascinated by this tool that I decided to become a certified trainer, and it became an important part of what I'm doing now.

PCM decodes human behaviour and explains how the process of communication operates for the six different personality types. These personality types are as follows:

- Thinker

    Applies logic and a structured approach in organising work and life, is responsible and has excellent time management skills.

- Persister

    Shares opinions freely, is conscientious and believes that dedication to one's values is essential in life.

- Harmoniser

    Approaches others and situations in a warm and compassionate way. Brings empathy and harmony to relationships at work and at home.

- Rebel

    Radiates a good mood by being spontaneous and playful. Can find creative solutions where others see problems.

- Imaginer

    Unfolds an internal universe of imaginations and hypotheses, is introspective and has a calm manner.

- Promoter

    Thrives on challenges and can adapt quickly to changing situations. Has a great deal of charm and can persuade people by being to the point and direct.

The good news is that everyone has all of these personality types within them and can communicate and connect with people who are different. The bad news is that a person can also be unconsciously set in their ways and not have much energy available to deal with those who are different. My passion, that I utilise in my PCM trainings, is for each person to become aware of their potential and how they can practice it by means of communication.

PCM gives you hands-on tools from the minute you walk out of the door from a training course and enables you to connect with people more effectively. PCM coaches are able to motivate people on a different level than the usual method of just telling them what to do in different situations. PCM is especially beneficial for executives and managers to cope with the accelerated speed of the current business world.

I was particularly intrigued with the different forms of predictable, sequential and measurable distress behaviour of the six personality types. Identifying these distress behaviours enabled me to objectify my own personal difficult situation. It also showed me what battery charges I have to give myself and what personal needs to fulfil in order to be a balanced human being. Working with PCM changed the world for me, and I believe for my clients as well.

Another important *aha* moment was when I got in touch with healing techniques based on shamanistic methods with scientific backing. I would say I'm starting to get glimpses into what the human brain can achieve and the capacity it has to develop. This has changed my view on mindset dramatically, and I know there's so much to explore for us humans. I find this topic absolutely fascinating.

Ilona Vass

What is your big WHY?

Getting the answers as to why the human race never stops hurting each other, so we can find ways to change the situation. With so much cruelty and violence that still exists on this planet, I'm not satisfied with answers like, "That's just how it is" and "That's human nature." Perhaps I'm just too much of an idealist to accept it. I believe it wouldn't be so difficult to channel negative energies into something productive and positive. People just need to get the right toolbox and know how to use it in ethical ways. I don't know why it's not happening faster, so I try to do my share in this lifetime to change the situation.

What do you think is your life purpose?

I believe it's changed over the years. Right now, being middle-aged, I'd say that in addition to raising a boy to become an emotionally mature male, it's to accompany and assist people to feel confident when handling difficult and challenging situations. I'd love to see people flourish, knowing they always have something in their toolbox they can use to help themselves and others through difficult times. I encourage everyone to continue to expand this toolbox and always be on a quest to improve their knowledge and awareness. It's most rewarding when my clients tell me they were able to handle a difficult situation better due to what they learnt in my training courses and coaching.

How are you currently making a difference in people's lives?

With my company, Dancing with the Dragons. The portfolio of services I offer gives me the daily opportunity to assist and accompany people and equip them on their journey to a better life. PCM allows people to understand where the other person is coming from, especially in stressful situations such as when there's shouting, manipulating, blaming, over-explaining, justifying, and crusading. PCM helps them to react in an appropriate way the personality type requires, as well as provide them with a feeling of relief when they understand they don't have to take on the behaviours of others.

Knowing how to avoid drama and not getting sucked into non-productive conversations makes a person feel powerful. This knowledge does help immensely in reducing the pain, stress and frustration that can be caused by human interaction. It's an excellent position to be in, and work from, when managing difficult situations. You can detox communication.

Besides introducing PCM in my trainings, coaching is hugely rewarding for me. Helping people find a way to achieve tasks, goals and dreams, is satisfying. Accompanying them as they take baby steps, which are actually huge changes, and realising how life-altering they are, helps me to know I chose the right path in being there for others. Baby steps create confidence and smoothes the path for bigger steps.

I also do inter-cultural consulting work. I'm familiar with the Chinese culture, due to my university degree and the many years I've lived and worked in China. I can read, write and speak fluent Mandarin. This type of work allows me to increase people's tolerance and build up curiosity for other possibilities as to their current procedures. I can help companies align their business endeavours with the right mindset and cultural understanding.

Last but not least, I lecture undergraduates on business subjects like global trends and cross-cultural management at a tertiary educational institution. I'm told my lecturing approach is engaging, and I fulfil my own wishes when I assist young people to learn important skills for life much earlier than I did.

What are you passionate about?

I'm passionate about what concerns my business and the work I'm doing, but I also have private passions.

Ilona Vass

I love any form of dance. To me, dance allows people to unconsciously express their true self in a safe way. Dancing connects you to your soul on a deep level. As a child, I learned ballet. I continued in high school with ballroom dancing, and I especially loved that and the Latin-American style. Later on at university, I practiced *Bharatanatyam*, which is a classical dance from India. I'm proud to say I've publicly performed both ballroom dancing and *Bharatanatyam* for many years and incorporate certain elements in my work as trainer and lecturer, which my clients and students love.

When I still lived back in my home country of Austria, one of my coaches pointed out to me that whenever I talked about dance, there was a shift in my entire body. He said my posture changed, the light in my eyes intensified and my energy visibly rose. He told me to tap into that exact feeling and energy when I managed staff and work engagements. It took me by surprise then, but it stuck with me.

What do you think people's biggest issues are?

That's a really big question, as it puts all people into one pot. I think different cultures and countries have different issues, but I'd say the biggest one is that people feel overwhelmed with the accelerated speed of everything that happens. Technological and digital developments, work expectations, increased competition on a global basis, and relationships. I believe that feeling overwhelmed in so many aspects of life takes people out of their true connection with themselves, which means they're frustrated and desperate. They're lost in their search to feel content and fulfilled. With this overload of information, they've been caught in a downward spiral and find it hard to pull them themselves out of that vicious cycle to push up again.

What's the best way to help people with this issue?

The best way to help is to first give them the power to believe in themselves and then to acquire a set of tools that will teach them to regain confidence, so they can keep up with the pressures of modern life. Tools that inspire them so much, they continue to use them. Simplicity and applicability are my key words!

How did you become interested in personal development?

I got in touch with soft skill training in my first career in aviation. I had a visionary and progressive boss at that time who enabled his team to get external training courses. This included a module-based certification course in organisational development and human resources. Within this program I had to design an emerging leader program and implement it into the organisation. It wound up being successful and extremely rewarding, not to mention how happy I was in my job at that time.

I was fascinated with this different type of training. Up till then I'd only experienced professional skills-based trainings. The benefits I had in my career through the soft-skills training were obvious, and I started to gain insights into myself and who I really was. It taught me how to be a better leader/manager.

Ever since, I've never stopped expanding my horizons in the field of human relations and self-development. Towards the end of my career in aviation, it became clear to me this was something I wanted to explore. I wanted a new career giving people another kind of training and support that had incredible benefits not only for business, but also for people to reconnect with themselves and live a fulfilled and content life.

What's your approach to the delivery of your training and coaching?

My chief aim in the training and coaching I deliver is that it be practical and simple. In so many corporate trainings, people are served with an overload of information, and it's trusted they will automatically transfer all of the delivered content into the workplace straight away.

This is not the case.

To really assist with the integration of the new material, it's necessary to facilitate a behavioural change. One way to do that is to work with instant, practical applications during the training. For example, as a second step I finish the PCM training with a personal action plan that motivates the client. It holds them accountable and lets them achieve and celebrate the results. As a third step, there's an after-course program component that gives the client the opportunity to reinforce the behaviour change. Ideally, the whole process of sustainable change is concluded with a few one-on-one coaching sessions to ensure the best outcome for a behaviour change and to imbed the learnt skills into their everyday work and personal life.

I provide a range of exercises, role-plays and simulations in my trainings, especially with the PCM trainings. It's so important to feel it when trying out different communication channels that cater to different personalities or when managing the distress behaviour of another person and bringing them back into a productive space. This goes beyond the usual "This is what you say in this situation, and that is what you do in that situation." PCM allows you to instantly act on the individual's behaviour and their personality.

As I said, every person has all six personalities inside of themselves to a different extent. The logical mind understands the theory of PCM rather quickly, but the real art is to feel and then practise your authentic self with those six different personalities. I also set up an action plan with my clients, to ensure they stay in the energy and are able to communicate successfully with people who have these different personality types.

I have a few coaching sessions with my clients to follow up with them on these action plans and fine-tune their strategies. This approach has shown excellent results for individuals and businesses.

What courses have you taken that enabled you to get started, or build upon, your business?

I've spent a long time feeling doubtful about having my own business. I had a wonderful corporate career and worked for a company with an excellent internal and external culture. This career ended when I went on maternity leave and stayed on in Australia. During that time I attended a course sponsored by a foundation that assisted women with children to set up their own business. The course started to build my confidence and gave me a nice initial boost. I'm still learning how to do it better and have discovered that the courses offered at Authentic Education to be outrageously fantastic and insightful.

As a certified PCM provider, I'm always attending professional development workshops. I also work internationally with other PCM trainers. This builds my business beyond Australia, and it's so delightful, as it proves to me that PCM is a truly intercultural tool that's applicable to everyone, regardless of their culture. I also deliver PCM in Mandarin in China, mainly for international companies with subsidiaries or joint ventures there.

I have three different coaching qualifications. Two of them fall under the category of results coaching and one specialises in learning transfer. In my business, coaching is not only an excellent stand-alone product, but it also combines well as a follow up to the PCM seminars and leadership trainings I offer. It assists people to have a high-quality outcome.

Beyond those core competencies, I've done numerous courses in sales, leadership and communication, which are also the foundation of my business.

Ilona Vass

Why is mindset important?

Mindset is a powerful force in life. Brain research is just starting to scratch the surface of what the human mind is actually capable of. It's fascinating and in my opinion should be a main subject taught at schools. Mindset has a major influence on a person's reality and can be trained. I like this saying by Anaïs Nin: "We do not see things as they are, we see things as we are." So why shouldn't people learn early in their education how to train their mind for their own benefit?

Mindset has the potential to improve quality of life and help you help deal with the pain different situations can create. It's important to understand how the mind can often trick you, so you can train it to see the good in every situation

How do you start your day?

I believe how you start and end your day are equally important. My daily do-me-good routine is split into mornings and evenings.

In the mornings I sit up in bed and spend ten-twenty minutes on mental exercises like meditation and heart breathing. Then I "listen" into my personality. I imagine a six-story house representing the six personalities defined in PCM, with each being a different level of energy. This is when I set myself up for being fully open for people with different personalities.

Then I imagine myself as a successful trainer and coach. This practice is called *Imaginaction*. After getting up I immediately drink a glass of water with a bit of freshly squeezed lemon juice, and just before eating a healthy breakfast I drink a bit of water with apple cider vinegar to boost my metabolism. Then I'm ready for the day.

In the evenings before I turn off the lights, I mentally go through everything I'm grateful for in life and what happened during the day.

This can include challenging situations. I do this until I feel joyful and warm and have a smile on my face. If I feel tired, drained or not my usual self, I incorporate other shamanic techniques into my routine to help my body and soul recover. Regardless, I try to do this once a week.

What are some tools or strategies you could recommend for keeping a balanced life?

One of my mottos in life comes from *Star Trek*. I embrace "infinite diversity in infinite combinations." Although in my work as a trainer and coach I teach various models and structures, I encourage participants not to box, categorise or stereotype people or cultures. I try to create an openness that allows enjoyment of the uniqueness of everyone. This helps maintain balance and grounding. It avoids the attitude of thinking a situation can only be handled one way and avoids preaching and imposing beliefs on others.

Another tool to keep balance in life is to ask core questions when your distress behaviour is showing. If you have the feeling you're not on top of your life anymore, and people and situations start to bother or charge you, asking yourself a core question can help you to rebalance, accept the negative feelings and return to your okay space.

For example, when I get angry and frustrated, such as when I'm in my car and my fellow drivers go too slow or don't indicate when they're going to turn, I always say to myself, *What is it I'm not seeing?* This question allows me to step into the bigger picture again, and even into someone else's perspective. That's often all it takes to get me back on track.

When I started to learn PCM, I got some useful insights as to what I have to do to charge my batteries. Another way to say it is I learned how to feed my psychological needs to stay motivated and communicate well. In the past I didn't really know how powerful this knowledge was for my wellbeing, and I think many people don't know it at all. Everyone has subconscious needs, and they vary from each of the six personality types. If you don't know how to meet them in a healthy way, you start to look for negative ways. This can lead to many difficulties in life. In all of my PCM courses, the participants work out an action plan about how to charge their batteries in their own best way.

Since I know what I have to do on a daily, weekly and monthly basis to keep me motivated, it's made me a much more balanced human being.

What are your favourite ways to relax and enjoy life?

My favourite ways to relax are very much linked to what PCM calls sensory stimulation. I enjoy being in nature with a focus on sensations. For instance, feeling the breeze on my skin, hearing the sound of water, seeing the light falling through leaves, smelling the damp aroma of moss after a rainfall or mushrooms about to break the surface. These sensory stimulations trigger memories, and I enjoy this way of revisiting glimpses of my past life. I've actually stopped running in nature, because it didn't allow me to experience all of these sensations. I realised running is great for my sports ambition, but it didn't charge my batteries in the way I need it to, so I prefer walking now.

I also love travelling with my son, preferably to warm climate zones, for exactly the same reasons. I enjoy different cultures and learning about their food habits.

Another way I have of relaxing is engaging in physical exercise where I strive for elegance and precision, not speed or competition. My favourite form of exercise is called Body Combat, which is a gym class with music and various martial arts designed and choreographed into combined movements. Body Combat is a non-contact way of doing martial arts and pushes cardio and core strengths. It's close to dance in its elegance, choreography, strive for technique and perfection, which I love. It's also a good substitute for dance, which I can't do at the moment. I'm working on a project called "Getting dance back into my life" for 2017. Every year I try something new at the gym and restructure my routine, but Body Combat is always part of it.

Does technology help or hinder?

Technology, and its development over the past fifty years, is incredibly fascinating. When I think back to when I was a university student and went with my sister to buy my first PC to type our master's theses, and what you can do today with just a mobile phone, I'm amazed by the developments that seem to operate at an exponential speed. This technological digital revolution, entering its fourth stage, is challenging for many people. If it helps or hinders depends upon how it's used.

It's unfortunate that many people will use it in non-productive ways that adds to what I call *information overload*. This information overload contributes to misunderstandings, misperceptions and misevaluations and doesn't improve communication in the sense of growing as human beings. Technology, used with positive meaning and an ethical purpose, can assist in dealing with the demands and the huge speed with which life goes nowadays.

One way of handling technology is to watch that you as a business owner or private citizen aren't contributing to the production of information overload. I believe it works best with the mindset of *less is more*. It's so tempting to use social media as an easy way of sharing and commenting, but it makes all the difference to double check and filter what you put out there.

It helps to give some thought beforehand if what you're publishing is assisting you in your purpose in life and if it's worth being your own personal message. You might be serving someone else's purpose by consistently sharing their messages, articles or sayings. Be picky with what you put out there. It will assist you in building the image you want to have, which is namely that of an elevated human being.

What does success mean to you?

You read about a lot about successful people who've "made it". Celebrities and other famous people who became wealthy can be an inspiration, and people admire them, but they seem to be in a different league. To define this as success is great, but it can make people stop seeing that success can be right in front of them, and it fosters the thinking of, *This is beyond my scope*. It just might require a different definition as to what success is, and it all becomes more tangible and in closer reach.

Success, to me personally, is when you're able to maintain your true self despite the challenges life can offer. It means managing your distress, and the negative or mask behaviour that comes with it, in a healthy way. It's remaining constantly curious about what life has to present as you strive to expand what you do and want to achieve. The people who put these techniques into practice are content, because they're clear about what they do and want and what they can give to other people.

Often these quiet achievers are the real inspiration, because they can make a tangible difference in the lives of others, as well as directly and indirectly instil the belief that success is achievable.

What can someone do right now to change their life?

I believe working with a coach can have an immediate impact on what that initial trigger change could be and to have a lot of stimulation and fun around putting ideas and plans to action. Despite being a coach myself and using self-coaching techniques, I totally enjoy getting coached, especially if I feel a bit stuck. Being coached always gives me this sensation of arriving at an insight and solution so much faster than by myself. Give it a try!

What are the best ways people can find energy?

PCM offers a great insight into your personality and what you have to do to be a centred and energetic human being. All six different personality types identified in PCM have a unique set of psychological needs, and there's no one-size-fits-all solution. That means you have to be really aware of who you are, and many people don't know how to charge their batteries and meet their psychological needs.

In my seminars, we develop a personalized action plan with each participant to make sure they can find energy and are ready to deal with challenges in a positive way. It's been a huge eye-opener for many of my participants, and they often say this was the best intervention they've had to feel more energised and happy with their life.

I also see the benefit of all kinds of mindfulness activities. I think it's best to look for activities that are simple and suit your personality.

 To discover more about how Ilona can help you *Elevate Your Life*, simply visit

www.elevate-books.com/life

Dianne Cao

Separation with Soul

Being in the first wave of Vietnamese refuge to arrive in Australia, Dianne Cao's formative years were spent in Penrith where she graduated as a pharmacist. Her transition to divorce coaching was inspired by her three children as she was going through a separation and divorce. It occurred to her that many women might be as discontented with life and living in ambivalence, just as she'd been. Dianne found a way to maintain a happy home during a difficult time and to make the process as seamless as possible, and she felt the need to share that information with others.

Dianne's goal is to help people find clarity within themselves, even when going through difficult times, and make authentic life decisions.

Dianne Cao
Separation with Soul

Please share a little about yourself.

I'm a mother of three and a pharmacist, currently partnered in three pharmacies. I came to Australia as a five-year-old refugee after the Vietnam War, the second child in a family of four. I grew up at the foot of the Blue Mountains where I attended Penrith High School, and although I didn't enjoy it, I performed reasonably well, became a pharmacist and ventured into business ownership.

I came to understand the meaning of choice early in life. The choice to want more for myself, to work hard at something if you want it bad enough, to keep going even the situation looks bleak, and above all, to be the best version of you, even when no one is watching.

The hurdles of life prepare you for the next race. I believe many hurdles have been thrown my way. Sometimes I'd trip over them, and at other times they'd sideline me. I'd sit and cry for a while, but I'd always get up and keep running. The approach I engaged to overcome these moments became my life strategies, and the insights that came from surpassing them are priceless. I now show them off proudly, like the battle scars of a warrior.

I love my coaching work that involves inspiring people to find balance in their life, to freely express themselves and to achieve their goals, while being congruent with their life's purpose. That's why I coach.

What's your definition of happiness?

My definition of happiness is finding the right balance between the body, mind and spirit. I think the body and mind belong to the egocentric self, while the spirit is obviously the spiritual self. Somewhere along the way, I got rather confused about what I'm supposed to be doing here. There was an internal voice and desire screaming out to me to do something else, which I believe is my spiritual calling. Then there was the physical world giving me the messages and values that define success, such as fame, fortune and physical attributes.

So, the way I made sense of it is with this formula: take the type of upbringing you had, add that to your inherent value, mix it with the opportunities you've been given, shake it up with the actions you've taken, and it will determine the type of life you currently have.

If you paid more attention to your ego-centred self, it's likely you've achieved some financial success and are comfortable financially, but you're searching for a deeper spiritual connection, meaning and purpose of life. However, if you've focused on your spiritual-centred self, at some point the cost of living in the physical realm will catch up with you, and you'll want more wealth creation strategies to balance it out.

The key is to find balance between the two selves but keep them running parallel with each other. Have a strong work ethic, positive values and finances. Set goals and be self-motivated to achieve them. Along the way, enjoy the journey and the people brought into your life. Find your spiritual truth while you're here, and be willing to learn the lessons in life you're supposed to, particularly the ones in the form of problems you can't seem to hurdle. Be authentic in all relationships, the most important one being with yourself, and leave this life knowing you've played the best game with the cards you were dealt.

What have you discovered is the best way to help your clients find balance?

The key is to be aware of when reality and expectations aren't correlating. That means expectations are unrealistic or what they're currently doing isn't serving their best interest. To determine what work needs to be done, the client identifies sectors of their life that need assistance. Setting goals, determining strategies and holding the clients accountable to this action plan are essential. My job as a coach is to be supportive, strong, resourceful and insightful in order to assist them in reaching their targeted goals. Of course, the final outcome and speed of results will be determined by the clients themselves. Learning coaching tools from Benjamin Harvey of Authentic Education was just what I needed. I felt his techniques were practical, simple and client focused, like "Be aware" and "Change is easy!"

What does being spiritual mean to you?

The Oxford dictionary defines it as *relating to or affecting the human spirit or soul as opposed to material or physical things*. The definition is so broad that everyone will delineate the concept differently. Some will define it as a religion, while for others it's a ritual or the meaning of life.

I define it as the deepest sense of life values, such as who we are, why we're here and how we live. It usually starts with a question, and it grows with time and experience. Life is a spiritual journey. Nobody is here to merely exist. Growing spiritually means feeling a sense of inner peace and connectedness. When events that happen to and around you align with your interpretation and how you feel, you're congruent. When you surrender and act mindfully because it's the right thing to do, without becoming attached to results, you free yourself from struggles, both internal and external.

I've heard people like Oprah and Ben Harvey describe life's lessons being sent in the form obstacles. It usually starts of as a tickle, a feeling that something isn't quite right. It tries to gain your attention. If you ignore it, a pebble is thrown your way. It hits you a bit harder to get you to address the message. If you still don't react, you get a brick thrown at you. If the brick doesn't get your attention, and you continue to ignore the message, a truck will hit you, and it will hit you time and time again until you do something about it.

These trucks, in my opinion, are lessons that need to be learned and can come in the form of a partner declaring they want a divorce, the electricity being cut off, getting evicted or a strained relationship with elderly parents. If you're aware, you can recognise these messages when they're in the form of a tickle or a pebble. Be intuitive enough to detect them early and act upon them. It's easy to blame your situation on external factors and slip into victim mode. There's usually a villain in the form of a boss, a terrible friend or selfish partner. However, to best serve your spiritual needs, just own the problem and work it through. In later stages these problems can seem like semi-trailers running you over. Wisdom and knowledge are only gained through the process of dealing with these obstacles.

What is your area of specialty, and why do you do it?

I believe I have solid values, a good moral compass and a strong work ethic. I did everything the ideal world, and Hollywood, presented to me as the ideal life. I didn't bully anyone in high school, befriended the lonely kids and championed the call of the underdog. I worked hard and saved, married a good man, had three children, ran a successful business, was filial to my parents, and always had good relations with my siblings and friends. I did all of the school mum activities, attended parents/teacher interviews and volunteered. Career wise, my husband and I were able to build a comfortable life for our family. However, I still felt unfulfilled. The blissful state that's supposed to happen once you've ticked all of the boxes, eluded me.

It was distressing to feel trapped in a life I'd created for myself based on external information about a desired lifestyle. What was more disturbing was that many looked at my life and thought it was ideal. That I had what a solid marriage should look like. From inside the marriage, I felt a slow and gradual death of my spirit. I was lonely. I saw my husband withdraw to the point he was just a body that went to work, came home and numbed himself on TV sport. Although we were both physically present, we'd checked out of our marriage and stopped sharing our dreams and passions. We were mechanical and pragmatic. I also noticed that the verbal conflicts were getting more intense, and we both became resigned and apathetic.

It was a gradual decline over five years, but after one of our explosive episodes, my husband and I decided to end the suffering for all involved. He's a private man who will not seek help or advice from anyone, so we navigated our separation by ourselves. Although trying at times, we both knew the process was based on getting the best outcome for our children. We wanted a win/win separation, because we still cared for each other, it's just that we disagreed on too many issues. We figured that even though our different core values and conflicting methodologies may have prevented us from becoming life partners, our children shouldn't have to wear our mistakes. We negotiated a peaceful, amicable, and dare I say, loving way to part. It felt right, and the conflicts subsided.

I later discovered that what we'd done was negotiate a parallel lives agreement. This is where we stayed together in the same house for the sake of the children and ran our successful business together, but had separate personal lives and friends. This isn't an ideal situation, nor is it normal, but it's working for us, and that's all that matters.

With my new circle of friends and acquaintances of divorced/separated people, I encountered betrayal, hatred, heartache, resentment, bitter family court battles and children caught in the crossfire. This intrigued me and made me want to find out about the divorce process and the best outcome given the circumstances.

More research unearthed *Consciously Uncoupling* by Katherine Woodward Thomas. It confirmed to me that what we did wasn't only mindful, it was created from a space of love and compassion. This is trending and is endorsed by celebrities like Gwyneth Paltrow and Chris Martin. A few years back, Demi Moore and Bruce Willis did the same thing.

After much research, I decided to qualify as first a coach and later a divorce coach with Certified Divorce Coach (CDC), run by Pegotty and Randy Cooper from Tampa, Florida, USA.

I slowly realised this could be my calling. I wanted to spend the rest of my life helping to ease the pain of divorce and minimise the impact on the children in the process. There are many marriages out there, each with varying circumstances and levels of dissatisfaction. However, at the heart of it are despondent people just looking for fulfilment and searching for that connection to their spiritual self. The divorce is just part of the process, but the consequences of a bad divorce can have major ramifications on those directly affected by it.

I've also written a mini e-book entitled *Parting Peacefully* that's easy to read and simple to follow. It may address some of your concerns about the journey of divorce. I initially discuss the institution of marriage, why a complete family is depicted as an ideal picture of happiness, how marriage has evolved to where it is now and the mindset behind it.

Then I walk you through the process of knowing exactly where you and your partner currently are, by helping you become honest with yourselves and express what you really want. You need to have integrity. If you can't ask for something, what's the chance of getting it? Understand where your partner is, and know for sure how committed they are and how much effort they're willing to contribute to achieve your goals. To help with the process, I've also enlisted relevant experts in their fields that include solicitors, psychologists, financial advisers and mediators.

Whether you want to reinvent a new and loving relationship with your current partner or believe the only way is out, I can guide you. Knowing exactly where you stand legally, what you're entitled to and the next steps to take, while having a clear map to your destination, allows you to be prepared for the journey and pre-empts the potential pitfalls. Then you can reach your destination with minimal cost, emotionally and financially. There's the physical process of separating, the chapter on parenting and the last chapter that covers the relationship you have with yourself, because once you get this right, everything else will fall into place.

I would like to share chapter four, the cooperative co-parenting strategy:

How to Navigate Co-Parenting the Complex Family

You will understand the importance of the concepts I've introduced, when you're living through the rest of your journey, especially in the parenting component.

If you've parted on good terms, you're moving on with your lives and are happy with the general direction your life is heading, it's easy to give and take. If need be, you'll organise and reorganise the arrangement so that both of your daily plans are catered for, while you share the process of shifting the children between the two residences and lives.

Your children are resilient, and they will adjust to this new situation. The physical adjustment is even easier when there's goodwill between the parents, and conversations between the two major figures in their lives are fluid and effective. You don't have to be best friends with each other (of course, if you can, that's great), but at least be on civil terms and behave with dignity. Your children see how you treat each other, and they will notice if you're displaying love and respect, even during difficult times, so try and be the best model you can to them. Show them divorce means Mum and Dad have decided not to be a couple anymore, but aside from that are still functioning beings and not individuals who've regressed into bickering, name calling and vengeful acts of aggression. It's important to limit the exposure they have to the conflict where possible. By providing a supported and safe environment, it allows them to adjust. Keep communication clear, and answer any questions they have with integrity and honesty.

Why the Solid Parenting Team is so Important

If you've read up on this subject of divorce, you might be concerned about studies that depict children of divorce with high levels of behavioural problems. How they suffer academically, are less likely to graduate from high school, are more likely to be involved in criminal activities, and are more inclined to engage in drug and alcohol use at an early age. Also, that the scars of the divorce remain with the child well into adulthood, resulting in poor relationship choices. However, you should note these statistics are based on outdated studies and the general model where the father leaves and has minimal interaction with the children.

In 1971, the late Judith Wallerstein, a psychologist and researcher, had a twenty-five year study of the long-term effect of divorce on the children that garnered her much criticism. She studied sixty divorced families and over a hundred children from middle-class Marin County, California, and concluded that children from divorced families were distressed immediately following the divorce, but the problems persisted even ten to fifteen years later. They became underachieving, self-deprecating and angry men and women who had a tougher time than most people in forming intimate relationships.

Wallerstein's study, although it yielded many useful insights, wasn't a hundred percent accurate due to her testing group. It was too small, and there was no variation in socioeconomic factors. However, it was a good basis for further studies. One from 2002, by psychologist E. Mavis Hetherington at the University of Virginia, found that many children experience short-term effects, especially anxiety, anger, shock and disbelief, but these reactions disappear by the second year. Only a minority of children suffer for a longer period of time. What researchers consistently found is that children who sustained more long-term effects experienced high levels of parental conflict during and after a divorce. Those who lived in a household with a high degree of discord can sometimes welcome the peace of a divorce.

Contrary to popular belief, children of divorce don't suffer psychological and emotional traumas. It's much worse for them to witness a broken marriage with the constant conflict and hostility that robs children of a peaceful home life existence. Their sanctuary is a battlefield. You're modelling the wrong type of relationship, and marriage is not supposed to look like that.

The late Kathleen O'Connell Corcoran, PhD, a senior practitioner, mediator and trainer from the USA, noted this in her article from June of 1997. She stated that researchers now view conflict, rather than the divorce or parenting schedule, as the single most critical determining factor in a child's post-divorce adjustment. The children who succeed after divorce have parents who can communicate effectively and work together. Kathleen's strategies to separate, remodel and maintain a healthy co-parenting strategy, allows both parents to proceed with effective parenting.

In her book, *Parenting with an Ex-Factor*, Jill Darcey spoke of her personal journey of successfully parenting three healthy and well-adjusted children with her ex-partner. A lot of it is practical and useful and gives great mindfulness advice. However, even if you know what to do, when flooded with emotions you may be unable to distinguish between pain that's a result of a past or present event. You're forced to decide and act from the primitive hind brain, and the actions derived from the fight-or-flight response aren't usually well thought out or highlight the best of who you are. In fact, it's usually your worst. That's why a coach during this phase of your life will prove invaluable. You have someone in your side pocket, calming down the emotions and helping to navigate the best path for you and your future.

Win/Win/Win Mindset

If you've separated and divorced amicably, the competent co-parenting strategies that will follow are practical, easy and logical for you. If the divorce was a blood bath, that's okay, too. You'll just have to try harder to overcome the emotional overwhelm. The key is to participate with the highest goal, that being the best outcome for the children and a win/win mindset. Whether it's who gets the children for the holidays, how you're going to celebrate your daughter's twenty-first birthday or "What are we going to do about Johnny's new friends? They seem really wild". Try to be accommodating, be mindful of each other's needs and back each other.

Raising teens, even in a nuclear family, is difficult in the current climate. The myriad of issues like peer pressure, identity and belonging, academic expectations, sex, drugs and alcohol, are common. Hence, in a complex family it's imperative that you don't leave the partnership vulnerable. More than ever, communication needs to be clear, and rules and structures need to be in place. You must be able to trust that your ex-partner will back you up in such situations. Both parents should try to cooperate in the best interest of the teen. Due to their need to test limits, teenagers will try many strategies from divide and conquer, to picking favourites, to tall-tales storytelling to get what they want. If they can see kinks in the armour, they will attack the weakest point.

At a time when you and your partner are both vying for their attention, try and put it all in perspective. If building a solid relationship with your teen means making demeaning or uncomplimentary comments about your ex-partner, then refrain from doing it. By voicing such unflattering comments, you're discrediting the value and worth of your ally. This other parent needs to have authority and respect to uphold the rules and pull in the reins when the children have gone too far. However, if you engage in undermining actions your teenager will see the potential to divide and conquer. They're smart enough to tell you why you're the better parent and how your ex-partner doesn't understand them, and soon they'll break down your boundaries.

However, if your children know the two of you do communicate regularly, the partnership is strong, and despite the divorce, the structures of the parenting team is solid, they'll feel safe to be teenagers by pushing boundaries and being met with firm but consistent resistance. They will learn that transparency and honesty are the only ways to build trust, which results in more privileges, and this is the normal process. Children with both parents residing in the same house will often experience the same issues, and it's all about pushing boundaries.

Sometimes the eldest child is the emotional crutch many single parents use to bounce ideas off and share their feelings with, which can range from the frustration of missing the bus that morning to being depressed and not able to get out of bed. This is a heavy load for any youngster to carry, no matter how mature they are for their age or how responsible they are in general. They're still children going through their own growing-up issues. It doesn't help if they now have to take on adult responsibilities and try and solve adult problems. By sharing such intimate and complex details about their other parent, what you may invariably do is alienate them against your ex, and you've robbed your children of one more person's love, along with the chance to build a relationship with their natural parent.

I'm not at all suggesting that you shouldn't ask your children for help. It's their obligation to contribute to the household chores and tasks to keep the home safe and running smoothly. Just don't tell them all of the emotional stuff they can't do anything about, thus making them feel helpless and powerless. Book a few sessions with a therapist to offload your emotions and a coach to get a strategy in place for moving you away from pain to a future you're excited about.

When You Remarry: The Role of the Stepparent

A complex family is one where both parents don't live under the same roof or there's a blended family with step children. Re-marriage has brought with it new dependents, and new parameters are sought to navigate these young individuals effectively to become healthy, inspiring adults.

Raising healthy and emotionally stable children has more to do with the ability of both parents being able to maintain a healthy partnership during the child's developmental stages than living under the same roof. Establishing parameters in step-parenting are also important to allow the absent parent to continue to contribute to the wellbeing of the child without undermining the position of the stepparent who cohabitates with them.

How do you facilitate a couple?

I have a questionnaire on the website that addresses emotional ambivalence. It's when you're in a state of uncertainty in your relationship, where it's not bad enough to want to leave, but not good enough to stay and remain blissful. The questionnaire seeks to give you clarity about your situation.

No one will know your unique circumstances better than you. If you think the relationship is worth saving, take the steps to make it better, attend relationship-building courses and work at improving it. If not, I have a four modules program where we talk about the process of divorce, knowing your legal rights, where you stand financially and how to have a peaceful resolution. Included with the course is a weekly session with your personal coach that will help you walk through this journey. Every divorce is as unique as a thumbprint, so we aim to coach you through the process. By the end of our program, you will have acquired the mindset and a game plan to walk through divorce with a win/win/win outcome.

The divorce process can be as smooth or as rocky as the couple would like it to be. Having an experienced and empathic divorce coach by your side to help you unravel the mess of divorce proceedings can calm the choppy waters.

Results in life start with a thought and then an action. Repeat. It's that simple!

Do you have any parting words?

I hope you've found some value in the information I've provided. If you were intrigued, agreed with or are curious about what else I do, please go to www.divorceandyou.com.au, and you'll find more information there.

I want to thank my friends and family for their presence and being part of this journey with me. For bringing the tickles, pebbles, bricks, and sometimes trucks, into my life. I'm sure I was one of those messengers for them as well. They've seen me at my best and surely at my worst.

The customers at my pharmacy affirm me every time they walk through my door and reengage with me. I love being of service and assisting them and their families. Their kind words, flowers and well wishes always bring a smile to my face.

And last, I'd like to send a friendly welcome to my future friends and relationships. I'm anticipating the challenges, the willingness to be open to new and exciting experiences and being humbled by others going through their own human experiences.

 To discover more about how Dianne can help you *Elevate Your Life*, simply visit

www.elevate-books.com/life

Mercedas Taaffe-Cooper
CounterPunch

Mercedas Taaffe-Cooper is a registered Psychologist (MSc Clinical Psych, APS), A Sports and Exercise Science graduate (BSc) and International Boxing Coach with over thirty-five years of coaching experience. Born in Coolaney County Sligo, Ireland, Mercedas's initial involvement in sports was with kickboxing, in which she won both European and World Championships. She's one of Ireland's most successful coaches and has worked with boxers who've ranked top ten in the world.

Mercedas moved to Australia in late 2006, and developed CounterPunch while completing her Master's research in Tasmania. Passionate about connecting with and enabling young people to reach their potential, Mercedas moved to the Northern Territory to work as a child and adolescent psychologist. It was there she piloted CounterPunch with the support of the Northern Territory Government (NTG) and the Menzies Centre for Child Development and Education.

Mercedas moved to South Australia in 2015 and lives in Mount Barker with her husband, Greg, a warrant officer in the Australian army.

Mercedas Taaffe-Cooper
CounterPunch

Physical activity-based solutions to connect, relate and communicate for positive mental health and performance

What's your biggest life lesson?

I used to think I was the only one who thought the way I did and felt as disconnected as I did, especially through my teenage years. Now I realise everyone has their own thoughts, feelings and insecurities just like I do. For me, connecting was the biggest step toward becoming truly happy.

Connecting on an emotional level is difficult, especially if you've learned not to trust or haven't developed an emotional vocabulary. Articulating feelings can be challenging. It's hard to connect with the world around you if you haven't learned to connect with yourself. The way I first connected with myself was physically. Exercise was my pill of choice.

Eventually exercise, specifically boxing, facilitated the connection between my mind and body, and ultimately connection with my spirit. My biggest life lesson is two-fold. First, I learned I needed to connect with myself before I connect with the world, and second, that the easiest way to make a connection is on a physical level. I've found this to be particularly true when connecting with young people.

How would you like to be remembered?

I would like to be remembered as someone who gave people a simple *how-to* system to be happy and realise their potential. A system that shows people how to connect first on a basic physical level, then ultimately on every level, and to especially let young people know they *do* have talent, they *do* have control and they *do* have a choice when it comes to living their life.

What message do you wish to share with the world?

Life is only complicated if you make it that way. Keep it simple. Also, you need to take control of your life and be responsible for your choices. Only then can you truly be happy.

The key for me in learning how to take control of my life was in understanding behaviour. Dr William Glasser defined behaviour in terms of *Total Behaviour*, which consists of what you think and do, and how you feel emotionally and physically.

He used the analogy of a front-wheel-drive car. The front wheels turn to when the steering wheel is turned, and the back wheels follow. The front wheels represent the *thinking* and *doing* components of behaviour, while the back wheels represent *emotional* and *physiological* feelings. For example, the emotional feeling of fear and the accompanying physical reaction of your heart beating rapidly.

In the same way the driver can only change the direction of the car by turning the front wheels, you can only alter how you feel by changing what you think and do. And you can't change the direction of your back wheels unless you first turn your front wheels, in the same way you can't change how you feel, either emotionally or physically, unless you first modify what you think and do.

In my experience, the main wheel to focus on is the *doing* wheel. The activity of thinking all by itself will not alter how you feel, unless you change what you do. Taking action, even the smallest step, is the key towards shifting how you feel, even if you don't know where it's transporting you. Taking action means taking control of your life and being responsible for your own happiness.

Mercedas Taaffe-Cooper

What's the worst thing that's ever happened to you, and how did you overcome it?

There were times in my life different situations seemed like the worst thing that could ever happen, but with the passage of time it all becomes relative. I've gained an appreciation and a new perspective from those experiences. I've learned that what doesn't kill you really does make you stronger.

Those experiences, and the lessons learned from them, have made me the person I am now. They've given me the passion that inspired me to create CounterPunch and the drive to help young people connect with themselves and realise their potential.

Have you had any aha moments that changed everything for you?

I've had lots of aha moments. In my teens I read a book called *Jonathon Livingston Seagull* by Richard Bach. I was raised a Catholic in Ireland, and while I had faith I never really connected with the whole religion thing. Reading this book was my first real connection with the possibility that there was something more. I had the realisation there were other possibilities, another level of existence, and that I can influence the path my life takes.

It took a number of years for me to see it, but now I know it was the first time I made a connection between the mind and body. For years, my focus was only on physical achievement. I was driven to challenge myself and achieve as much as I could. When I took up martial arts, I had a black belt within two years, I was a European champion in three years, and a world champion within four years. I trained to the point of addiction. But despite all of my achieving, I never really felt fulfilled.

Once I realised the potential of connecting mind and body, or connecting thinking with physiology, I became determined to learn as much as I could at an intellectual level. I studied, among other subjects, psychology, martial arts, boxing, sports and exercise science, energy healing and Reality Therapy/Choice Theory.

With all of this, it was perhaps inevitable I would become a psychologist, but my journey took a few scenic detours along the way. However, coaching is something I've done for a lifetime, and it's always been a deep passion of mine.

My next standout aha moment came when I first learned about William Glasser's contribution to Positive Psychology in the form of Choice Theory and its application, Reality Therapy. I'd won a scholarship to study a PhD in Sports Psychology at the University of Limerick, Ireland, the same institution where I'd gained my BSc in Sports and Exercise Science.

As part of my research, I needed to do some training in Choice Theory, and this training proved to be a major turning point in my life, so much so that shortly afterwards I gave up my 60,000 euro scholarship to do my PhD, sold the home I grew up in and set in motion my plans to immigrate to Australia.

That's how powerful this learning was for me. I've actioned the concepts I learned, and I know they work, because I've experienced the results for myself. For this reason, Glasser's ideas form a core element of my CounterPunch program.

What's the best thing that's ever happened to you and why?

Shortly after my move to Australia, I ended up in Tasmania and ultimately met my husband, Greg. Don't tell him, but yeah, I'd have to rate this as the best thing that's ever happened to me. The relationship we have has been the spiritual part of the linking of body, mind and spirit. He's the proof for me that connecting on an ethereal level, one of shared and compatible energy soul mates, is indeed possible. Mind you, if I mentioned to him anything about energy or other dimensions, he'd say I was nuts!

Mercedas Taaffe-Cooper

What do you believe you've been put on the planet to do?

I know it's strange, but despite having felt so disconnected, especially through my teens and twenties, I still felt like I was put here for a purpose. Now having turned fifty, I feel my purpose is much clearer. I believe the reason for everything I've experienced has been to share what I've learned to help teach others, especially young people, how to connect and realise their true potential, and ultimately how to be happy.

Connection has been a running theme through my life's journey. It's embedded in the creation, delivery and essence of the CounterPunch program, which connects all I've learned about psychology, boxing, sports science and Choice Theory into a program that teaches people how to connect, relate and communicate in order to be happy from within. It seems somehow like it was always destined to be.

Where did the name CounterPunch come from?

Counterpunch is a boxing term, but its connotation has a far wider application. In boxing, a counterpunch is a positive, thought-induced response to an attack, rather than a reaction. Life is a bit like boxing. The ring is your world, and your opponent represents the obstacles you face.

In life, as in the ring, you can react, or you can choose to respond. For me, CounterPunch is positive. It means to get around, find another way, punch through and be strategic. It implies choice, creating, enabling, reinforcing, the rewiring of neural pathways, creating new pathways, transference of energy, resilience, strength and determination. All of that applies to boxing and life. It's a powerful combination.

That's why I chose the name CounterPunch.

Why did you develop the CounterPunch program?

So much of life and learning is framed around negatives and conformity. Canadian Eric Wong, mixed martial artist and coach, refers to the behavioural expectations, the way you live your life and the way society expects you to behave, as *The Code*. The problem with this code is that it doesn't always give fulfilment. Instead, it leaves you feeling empty, so you distract yourself from this feeling by whatever means necessary.

For many of the young people I've worked with in my thirty-five years of coaching, I've discovered this distraction took the form of alcohol, drugs, gangs and other self-destructive behaviours. Anything that could give fulfilment, however brief. If it wasn't distracting or fulfilling enough, isolation, depression and ultimately suicide was often seen as the solution.

Today, this Code is perpetuated in education and health. The focus is on punishment, not choice, sickness, not wellness. People fix a situation after the fact rather than provide the tools needed for prevention. There's a reaction to crises and not a response to needs.

There are some fantastic schools and wonderful teachers. I've met many in my work, but for the most part they're limited by the system within which they have to operate. For some students this system works, possibly even for the majority. However, the fact remains that one system won't work for every student.

> "Everybody is a genius, but if you judge a fish by its ability to climb a tree it will live its whole life believing it is stupid."
> ~ Albert Einstein

Mercedas Taaffe-Cooper

Imagine if the school curriculum taught young people how to meet their needs effectively, create good relationships, develop and maintain resilience and self-esteem, be responsible for their choices and be proactive in their own wellbeing. Imagine if schools had more options when trying to connect with students, especially those whose code is not fulfilled by the current system. What if they supplied options that don't punish but instead give real, active and inspiring alternatives?

This is why I'm so passionate about creating real change for those whose needs aren't being met, by providing an appealing, proactive alternative. It's why I developed CounterPunch. I saw a need for other options to connect in a positive and fun way. Too many students aren't getting what they need from the system, despite the many wonderful people who work in it. Mental health issues are prevalent, as are negative and aggressive behaviours, which is highlighted by the prevalence of incidents involving deadly, unprovoked one-punch attacks. In the last fifteen years, body image issues have become statistically four times more prevalent, for both males and females.

Young people are being labelled more and more as troublemakers, useless, stupid or diagnosed as depressed or psychotic. Then they wind up owning those labels into adulthood. Many young people are simply trying to connect. They just haven't learned how. The purpose of CounterPunch is to help show them how to connect.

How can CounterPunch help people to connect?

Young people connect in a different way from adults. As a therapist I've worked with both, and what I've discovered is that adults are content to sit face to face and use talk therapy. They maintain good eye contact. Young people, on the other hand, at least in my experience, don't like this method. Talk therapy can often take the form of intermittent grunts and rushing out the door at the first opportunity. While working as a school counsellor in Ireland, I discovered I needed another plan if I was going to connect and be more effective with my young clients.

My solution was the genesis of CounterPunch.

I decided to develop what I knew worked for me. Throughout my teens and twenties, as I mentioned earlier, physical activity was my addiction. My way to break The Code and feel fulfilled, at least at a physical level. My original career in martial arts had by now specialised into boxing. I seemed to have an aptitude for it and made it my focus.

My training in Reality Therapy illustrated for me that in order to connect there must be a balance of power to counteract the power need. (See below). Glasser explains behaviour in terms of inbuilt genetic needs you're born with. Behaviour is driven by the need you perceive as not being met at that moment in time. Glasser identified these as:

- the need to belong, to connect to others, and to love and be loved (Love & Belonging)
- the need to feel powerful, significant and competent (Power)
- the need for freedom and autonomy (Freedom)
- the need to have fun and continue learning (Fun)

In my years working with young people, I invariably found that the power need was the biggest factor driving their behaviour. Glasser says it's not about having power *over* someone. It's about the power within you. What gives you intrinsic satisfaction? What can you do that's in your control and doesn't depend on anyone else or hurt anyone else if you do it? Finding a hobby, taking up sports or being creative, such as playing an instrument, painting or writing, were often all the intervention required for the young people I've worked with to meet their power need and for changes in behaviour to occur.

When you think about it, you realise the school system is an imbalance of power. The teacher instructs, and the students follow instruction. They get told where they need to be, what time to be there, when they can eat, when they can play and what they should wear. They have little input in the decision-making process. This imbalance of power tends to put the student on the defensive. However dominant the system may try to be, students will hold on to their power as tightly as they can to maintain their individuality.

> "The Individual has always had to struggle to keep from being overwhelmed by the tribe. To be your own man (or woman) is a hard business. If you try it you will be lonely often and sometimes frightened, but no price is too high for the privilege of owning yourself."
> ~ Rudyard Kipling

This striving to maintain power will, by definition, make young people resistant to connection, particularly in the school setting. This is especially true for those kids for whom The Code doesn't give fulfilment.

I discovered that giving my client a pair of boxing gloves, a little instruction on correct technique and holding a set of focus pads for them to punch, was a wonderfully effective way to level the playing field. Five minutes of hitting pads progressed our relationship more than many hours of talk sessions. Giving them permission to hit something was like unplugging a gusher. The relief was palpable. There were instant smiles and questions. It satisfied their power need, and a powerful connection was made.

I drew two conclusions from this experience. First, when working with young people, doing an activity is a much more effective way to meet their needs than just talking, and second, physical exercise, specifically boxing, is a hugely powerful medium of connection.

It was while completing my thesis research for my Master's degree in Clinical Psychology at the University of Tasmania that I got to formally research my conclusions. In 2006, while still in Ireland, I was fortunate enough to co-author a Reality Therapy-based workbook called "In the Driving Seat". I decided to pilot this program for the research component of my master's degree. The program consisted of teaching a sixth grade class the components of Choice Theory once a week, over a twelve-week period.

It was in a classroom setting, and it was a crowded classroom, so the opportunity to incorporate an exercise component was somewhat limited. I did, however, change the physiology of the participants through the use of *kiai*, which is basically a breathing technique, combined with a loud roar from the base of the diaphragm on exhalation. This proved a source of great elation for the participants, and the feedback proved to me the value of changing the physiology in facilitating connection. Imagine the impact if the physical component could be incorporated to a greater degree.

Why did you choose Boxing?

I chose boxing for a number of reasons. I believe it's a perfect analogy for life. The boxing ring is your world, and your opponent represents the obstacles you face in your world. My own area of expertise is boxing, and it's the physical medium I understand best. I know boxing works, because I've experienced the positive results of using it both as a participant and coach.

Numerous articles, documentaries and even movies have highlighted what those of us in the business have always known, which is that boxing is a tremendously powerful medium to help young people stay on the straight and narrow. The *Rocky* movie series, although fiction, emulates the powerful mentoring relationship between boxer and coach. Perhaps the connection is so unique because it's a combat sport, and there's no room for any pretence. It's real.

Mercedas Taaffe-Cooper

> "Few places in life breed absolute truth like the boxing ring. Any fighter can speak big, but in the ring there is no way to avoid the evolution of reality."
> ~ *Vivek Wallac*

I believe boxing is such a powerful medium to connect with young people. It creates mutual trust, allows a physical expression of emotion and teaches control. It's attractive to young people, because they get to actively participate. It's a positive psychology.

The technical and tactical components provide perfect analogies for teaching techniques and tactics for life. For example, boxing is a dance. It teaches you to ground your feet, create stability and transfer energy from the ground through your core and out through your extremities. It powers the body to punch through and centres the mind to think clearly. Grounding of feet and clarity of thinking are often what young people need more of in their life.

Boxing is a physical challenge, and progress can be measured. For many of the hundreds of young people I've coached over the years, I've discovered the competitive pathway has provided a positive and constructive way for them to meet their power need. I've observed a direct parallel between growth and progression in skill level with growth in confidence, resilience and self-worth. Mastering the technical stages of progression in boxing gives participants the chance to experience success, and with the experience of success comes the development of confidence.

Many of the CounterPunch graduates don't choose to compete but nonetheless show the same parallel progressions as they learn the skills of boxing. Their increased confidence is accompanied by improved relationships and development into young leaders and mentors in their schools and wider communities, thus broadening the impact and benefits of the program.

Combining sports psychology and Choice Theory with sports, exercise science and boxing, provides a complete package in helping young people to get on track and reach their potential for happiness. By giving boxing legitimacy in the education and health system through the addition of an empirically based behavioural change program, I hope to provide the answers schools are seeking in terms of strategies to connect with young people for whom The Code is not enough.

Can CounterPunch be used with other sports?

Yes, absolutely. The CounterPunch curriculum can be delivered using other sports. I chose boxing simply because it's the sport I know best, and I love to use it. When selecting what sport to use, I recommend you keep the following in mind.

The sport must allow physical expression to empower and engage but also emphasise the importance of control. The technical phases of learning need to provide ample opportunity for participants to experience success and develop trust. Most importantly, participants should want to participate in the sport. This initial attraction to the cool image boxing has among youth is often a key first step to engage. It's important that whatever sport you choose can sell itself to the young people you target.

It also helps if the sport is adaptable to different environments. The first time I used boxing as a medium, it was in an area the size of a cloakroom. Also, the less equipment required, the more adaptable it will be. Gloves and focus pads are quite portable.

I believe the analogies I use between boxing and life are easily transferable. To do so will require a level of technical knowledge of the chosen sport. For example, the grounding of feet and transference of power, as well as other parallels I use in the CounterPunch curriculum, could be applied across a wide range of sports.

How is CounterPunch delivered?

The purpose of CounterPunch is to provide a teaching tool that fulfils the objectives I've already outlined. It needs to be a curriculum that teaches young people how to meet their needs, create good relationships and develop and maintain resilience and self–worth. It should also show how to be responsible for their choices and be proactive in their own wellbeing.

Counterpunch is a tool that gives schools, or any agency that works with youth, an effective option to connect with students, especially those who may be struggling to reach their learning potential. The CounterPunch curriculum is designed to easily fit with national curriculum standards for education, and in its purest format is delivered over the school year in three phases, which are:

▶ Phase 1: Stepping into the ring

- Learn the basics of physical preparation, physiology and boxing technique
- Nutrition
- Lifestyle education.
- How to set and achieve value-linked goals.
- Problem solving and having fun doing it.

▶ Phase 2: Mastering your ringcraft-develop your CV.

- The performance jigsaw

- The 4 C's of mental fitness
- Techniques and tactics of boxing
- Techniques and tactics for life
- How to use values to change behaviour

▶ Phase 3: Master your self

- How to feel good.
- Change your physiology
- Clean the windscreen
- Change your perspective
- What makes you behave the way you do?
- What do you need?
- What's important to you?
- Who's the boss?
- Make the change

One of the key benefits of the CounterPunch program is its flexible application. It can be delivered for one hour a week over twenty weeks as part of a school curriculum, or as a two or three day intensive program for teachers, coaches, parents, corporates, agencies, businesses or any groups who work together and want to connect, relate, communicate and have fun doing it. A *train the trainer* option is also available to allow teaching staff, youth group workers, team managers or club coaches to become certified CounterPunch deliverers.

Mercedas Taaffe-Cooper

You can see a video of CounterPunch in action by following this link:

https://youtu.be/py1I9BPDYDl

Preview: YouTube video CounterPunch in Action

Has CounterPunch made a difference in people's lives?

Feedback on the impact of the CounterPunch program from students, teachers, school principals, school psychologists, adult participants and parents has been extremely positive. Here is just a sample.

> "CounterPunch saved my Life."
> ~ *Ash, a participant in the first-ever CP Program in 2011/12*

"It came across as a lot more motivating than other stuff. It made me more determined to achieve my goals."
~ *Kody, CP participant in 2012/13 and National Junior Bull Riding champion, 2013*

"Great for my focus and confidence. Taught me self-discipline. It helped me in pretty much everything at school when I moved interstate."
~ *Connor, CP participant, 2012/13*

"It gave me skills for day-to-day life. I now understand that if I take a certain path it has a consequence, but I now know that I have the power to choose the consequence by choosing the path. I am in control."
~ *Trey, CP Young Leader program and 2014 National Junior Boxing champion*

"CounterPunch has been a valuable addition to our student learning and wellbeing. Students are motivated and have developed some really positive decision-making skills at school, at home and in the community."
~ *Sarah, School Principal*

"I was really impressed with the delivery. I availed of the professional learning and have found it invaluable to me as a teacher. I continue to implement this learning at school on a daily basis."
~ Reg, Teacher

"I love the evidence-based nature of the program and the ease with which it can be built into students' educational programs (or company protocols). The individual benefit for participants far exceeded my expectations. As a school we have seen reduced suspensions, increased attendance, improved social and emotional wellbeing and improved interpersonal relationships, both at home and at school. CounterPunch has become a core element of our school-wide wellbeing program that has proven effective in all aspects of students' lives."
~ Beth, School Psychologist

"As an adult participant, I have witnessed and experienced the positive outcomes that CounterPunch encourages and provides. I achieved my goals, both fitness and personal."
~ Lloyd, Adult participant 2014

"As a parent, I highly recommend CounterPunch. As an army member, I've moved from post to post with my family, so my son has had to change schools and peer groups regularly. CounterPunch came at a great time for my son. It was a great boost for him and reinforced his respect for self and others. His fitness, strength and self-confidence grew weekly, and this transferred into other areas in his life. My son accredits CounterPunch with having set him up for his current school and sporting endeavours and life in general."

~ Scott, Parent

"CounterPunch changed my son's life completely. It has increased his self-esteem hugely, helped him overcome anxiety and fear, and exhibit tolerance and empathy. He has ceased all medications and counselling, obtained his driver's license and is making a key contribution to his family and community"

~ Keith, Parent

"Just wanted to share the impact of your two-hour CounterPunch presentation. Everyone has incorporated something of what you presented into their own training. They just love what you presented and talk about it often. Thanks again."

~ Jan, Boxing Coach

Mercedas Taaffe-Cooper

> "I have been involved with the Counterpunch program for the last four years. During this time I have seen the growth in the students in their attitude and decision making. The practical section of CounterPunch was easy for the students to understand, as it was explained using language the students could identify with. I have had numerous parents comment on the positive change they have noticed in their child and accredit Counterpunch to their change in behaviour."
> ~ *Karen, Student Liaison Officer*

What would you like your legacy to be?

I would love to see CounterPunch incorporated as part of the national standards school curriculum and used by all who work with youth and are passionate about seeing them realise their potential to be happy and fulfilled.

My vision is to create change through a system that has been developed to engage, empower and connect youth to reach their full potential. With the boxing ring being their world and the opponent their obstacles, they learn strategies to take control of their life, be responsible for their choices and be the master of their own happiness.

 To discover more about how Merc can help you *Elevate Your Life*, simply visit

www.elevate-books.com/life

Rebecca Jones
Goals for Grief

Rebecca Jones is a respected life coach who gained her qualification from Authentic Education in Sydney, Australia. Her clients include those suffering from anxiety, depression and feeling stuck in life. She also helps people who've experienced domestic violence, childhood abuse, bullying, molestation and unresolved grief.

Rebecca is most proud of helping people stuck in their pain to move forward and have a sense of peace about their past and an eagerness to experience what lies ahead. She loves watching her clients transform.

Rebecca now lives in Melbourne, where she works as a life coach and uses powerful tools to help her clients move forward in life.

Rebecca Jones
Goals for Grief

What's the worst event that has ever happened to you, and how did you overcome it?

The death of my older sister, Tahnee, when I was seventeen years old.

It was confronting seeing my parents heartbroken, having to bury their eldest daughter. My brothers and I were devastated and lost without our sister. We were all broken yet trying aimlessly to console one another, while navigating our way through the unfamiliar territory of grief, loss and pain so intense and debilitating, it felt impossible to function.

Returning to school was difficult. I no longer fit in with my friends. Nor did I have any desire or interest in doing so. I had good friends, but I eventually withdrew so much I lost them one by one, including a relationship I was in at the time. I cried myself to sleep every night for two years after her death.

I joined a support group for young, grieving people, which helped me. As I struggled enormously to connect with my friends at school, I found it liberating connecting with others from the group who were going through the same experiences, emotions and struggles as I was.

At nineteen, I enrolled in a massage course that gave me a little bit of purpose. This was the beginning of my turning point. I was finally connecting again with likeminded people, and I believe the physical touch of massage I received every other day whilst I studied, helped me both physically and emotionally.

What also helped me was living with my brother abroad in Los Angeles for two months. All of my old memories connected to Tahnee were predominantly in my home and hometown. Back there, I felt like *sad, pathetic Bec*. In America I was introduced to new people who didn't know anything about me. Consequently, I felt free to be a new me who was, carefree and happy. This was enormously liberating.

In this new environment, I had no memories of Tahnee. I wasn't eliminating her from my life. I still thought of her every day and carried enormous grief, but I was removed from the places and situations that triggered extra sadness. This, combined with the enjoyment of exploring my new environment, allowed me to start letting fun back into my life.

Over the years, especially in the beginning, I did a lot of soul searching. I had many questions about life and death. In my quest for answers, I read books on near-death experiences. I looked at reincarnation, karma, and all sorts other philosophies to get answers. I kept searching until my situation made sense to me. Those answers are personal and possibly wouldn't even resonate with my own family members, but they worked for me. That was one of the biggest pieces to my gaining acceptance and peace to move forward in my life.

What would you say to someone who's grieving?

I could give many responses, but one incident stands out for me. When I was in year twelve in high school, a friend whose mother passed away several years earlier told me something rather profound not long after Tahnee died. She said, "It doesn't stop hurting, but it does get easier." I didn't really understand what she meant at the time, but I always remembered her words. Twenty years on, I think they're quite possibly the best words to describe grief. I'll add that the feeling of not knowing how to go on will subside, and one day you'll be able to watch the sun come up again and be happy you're alive to see it.

Rebecca Jones

How do you deal with anniversaries and special days?

In the beginning, I was a raw nerve. But in time it was like I was doing all right until an occasion like Tahnee's birthday would roll around. The wound would reopen, and I'd be taken to my knees again.

Sometimes the days that were crushing for me weren't obvious to others. For instance, turning the age Tahnee was when she died, or a year later when I became older than my older sister. Another time was the twenty-first anniversary of her death, because she'd been gone as long as she lived. You know they're gone forever, but sometimes you just wish you could have them back to breathe life into those few faded memories with their smile, laughter and mannerisms.

As the years went by, I decided to give myself two days a year to reflect and think about Tahnee and allow myself to just feel whatever I'm feeling. On those days, I pick one of our favourite movies and watch it while fondly remembering our favourite scenes and taking pleasure in the wonderful times we had watching them together. It has become my little ritual in recent years and makes me feel connected to her in a joyful way.

If Tahnee were alive today, I have no way of knowing what she would be doing with her life and how we'd spend our time together. I choose to never entertain such futile questions on a regular basis. However, on days like my birthday, Christmas, Tahnee's birthday and really special days when I'm with members of my family, I do think of Tahnee. I know that at some point during the day, I would have spoken to her or been with her. It's in these moments I still feel a pang of pain. I'll always love her and cherish having had her in my life, and it's because of the deep joy she bought me that I will no doubt always feel some moments of sadness she's not with us. I think that's okay. I still function on a daily basis. I'm a better person because of her, and I'm allowed to feel whatever comes up from time to time.

Do you believe in signs from the universe?

Yes, I do. Synchronicity, coincidence and signs. I believe there's something in the random and unexplainable.

An extraordinary coincidence occurred on the seventh anniversary of Tahnee's death, when my nephew was born. The most horrid of days for our family had turned into a reason to smile every year from that day forward, when we celebrate his birthday. A gift from Tahnee? Sheer coincidence? Who knows, but what a magical blessing it was to our family. Now on her anniversary we all have a reason to genuinely smile.

What are you most proud of?

My smile. When I was heavily grieving and depressed, people used to tell me to smile all of the time. It was infuriating. I hated it. I remember one time standing in front of the mirror and forcing a smile on my face before bursting into uncontrollable tears. I couldn't do it.

To this day when people comment on my smile or how smiley I am, I just love it. One time when I did split shifts on a mine site starting at 4:30am, there were several people who regularly commented on how great it was to see my smile each morning in a place no one wanted to be. One guy nicknamed me smiley. In another workplace, I had a boss make numerous remarks about my smile. Colleagues would ask what I was smiling about. It's not that I'm permanently smiling, but when I do receive such remarks, it delights me. For people to think of me as a smiley person when once I couldn't muster up one at all, is something I'm really proud of. It always reminds me of how far I've come.

How can people be happier?

Appreciation. The act of acknowledging and valuing what you have in your life.

I have immersed myself in many modalities over the years in my search for peace and inner happiness. It wasn't until I decided to make appreciation not only a part of my daily life, but the focus of my life, that change truly occurred. I've come to notice you can't feel dissatisfaction or sadness or frustration at the same time as appreciation. It's one or the other.

Appreciation, in my opinion, is one of the best, most simplistic and powerful ways to happiness.

How can people appreciate more?

The teachings of Abraham Hicks and Dr. John Demartini have influenced me the most in regards to appreciation. Abraham Hicks says to take several sheets of paper, write a different topic on each page, fill the pages with positive aspects about that topic and repeat daily.

Upon committing to these activities, I discovered I looked for people, places, and situations to appreciate. This is one way to create new neural pathways and to train your brain to think more optimistically.

Appreciation was so transformative for me that I've never stopped practicing it daily since I discovered its importance. I start and finish each day with appreciating thoughts, and I deliberately find people, places and situations to appreciate throughout every day. I'm a better, happier person for it.

What is your biggest life lesson?

Owning my self-worth. To feel it and know it. You start out by improving your self-talk, which in time will translate into knowing and feeling you're deserving of the life you want to live.

There are always stories of celebrities who seem to have it all: status, fame, amazing homes, jet-setting lifestyles, famous friends, gorgeous looks, beautiful people throwing themselves at them and everyone wanting to be their friend. Because the perception is that they have it all, it seems incredible they could possibly be unhappy, and why on earth would they be checking themselves into rehab?

However, when you don't feel good enough inside or believe you deserve those accolades, none of it will fill the void inside. I'm not talking about being egotistical, overtly proud or obnoxious. Just owning and knowing your intrinsic value.

What can someone do now to change their life?

Address their feelings and beliefs around their worthiness. There are several ways this can be done, but I'll suggest two methods that were of great help to me, because I believe they were the two most influential tools that created my transformation.

I always seek knowledge, especially from people excelling in areas I'm interested in. There was an awesome tip I received from Benjamin Harvey at Authentic Education. He said every day for three months I should write down a hundred reasons why I'm worthy or deserving of whatever it is I want. Try it! You may only think of fifteen reasons to begin with. See if you struggle with the exercise. It can be quite revealing. It does get easier with practice and repetition, once you allow yourself to see where and how you shine and add value to the lives of others.

You can do all of the personal growth and development in the world, but if you don't address your worthiness and honestly believe you're deserving of the life you're currently living or want to live, then you're going to experience a feeling of lack or misery. You risk giving somebody or something else the power to make you feel fulfilled.

On the flipside, you can have a wonderful life, surrounded by wonderful people but still feel empty inside. Having a solid sense of self-worth doesn't mean you won't ever feel pain, but you will be emotionally stronger when life's events don't go your way. You need to see and feel your own worthiness in life the way you see it in those you love most. You wouldn't treat or speak to someone you care about with contempt and criticism, so why do that to yourself?

The second method whereby I noticed change in my own worthiness was through certain hypnotic recordings. I know they worked, because I heard the words from the recordings being repeated in my mind and in conversations I had. I also saw changes in my behaviour. In situations where once I would have remained quiet and polite or allowed myself to be disrespected, I began voicing my opinion and standing up for myself. I even told certain people they could no longer speak to me disrespectfully, and that if they continued doing so, I would no longer have them in my life. It was so empowering, and it was the result of feeling my own worthiness.

Do you believe in the mind-body connection?

Absolutely, I do. People understand the concept of butterflies in the stomach or the heart racing when getting up to perform a speech, but unless the feelings are intense, they don't realise how directly linked the mind and body are. Through my treatments and training, I've witnessed many times where physical sensations are intertwined with emotions and events.

I once had a client with post-traumatic stress. I use a method called Faster EFT (Faster Emotional Freedom Technique). It incorporates tapping on specific Chinese meridian points whilst working on a charged memory or emotion in order to clear it. Whenever we'd do tapping work, she would instantly zone out so much that she would nearly fall asleep every time, regardless of how much energy she had before we started. She so desperately didn't want to go back to those memories, her body shut down to avoid it.

I had a client who was afraid of heights. We addressed a memory where she once fell from a height, and then I walked her through the feelings and sensations she felt when thinking about being up high. Once we did that, she was able to climb up on a ladder without any physical reaction at all.

The mind doesn't know if what you're thinking about is actually happening in the moment, a memory or a made-up image. The meaning you give an event will determine the way the body will react. It's no different from reminiscing about a special memory and feeling all blissed-out and calm. The body responds to the meaning given to the thought.

Although you may not be able to change your circumstances, you can change your attitude to what's happening. A good attitude will influence the body's response.

Why is mindset important?

Mindset is most important, in my opinion. Some of the most influential changes I've seen within myself have to do with addressing worthiness, feeling appreciation and having goals. However, these are all subheadings that go under the mindset umbrella. The reason I'm not who I used to be when I was struggling so much is because I no longer think the same thoughts.

Sometimes I gained perspective through life experience or conversation. Other times it was words in a book or a song and other times, again, it came from the love and support of someone special. However it happened, bit by bit, my beliefs got questioned, challenged, re-evaluated, changed or tweaked.

Looking back, without fail, I can say that as I received peace regarding the events in my life or experienced some kind of growth and change, it was always my mindset that changed. Mindset can imprison or liberate you.

Is there a difference between having a sense of purpose and achieving a goal?

These terms get used interchangeably. However, although similar, there is a difference.

Having purpose is the overall driving force behind action. It's the WHY. Purpose, to me, is more altruistic. It's bigger than we are. It's about service to others or the environment, and it comes more from inspiration.

Goals can relate to your purpose but not necessarily. They're what you want to experience or have. Goals can be big and grandiose like the ones on a bucket list or an ideal home, whilst others may be what you'd like to accomplish by the end of the week.

You can use goals to reach and achieve your purpose. For example, my purpose is to help people suffering emotionally to find peace and move forward in life. I aim to achieve this through my coaching, therapies and education. So for each area I've broken down the goals, but they still signify my overall purpose. I also have goals unrelated to my bigger purpose, such as my ideal relationship and the type of lifestyle I want to live.

I might be moving towards a goal, when I decide I no longer want it. As a result, I might tweak it or change it altogether. However, my sense of purpose has been unwavering over the years. If anything, it's just gotten clearer and more specific.

Is it important to set goals?

Absolutely.

Whilst my sister was alive, I was that young girl who upon seeing my first star every night would say out loud, "Star light, star bright, first star I see tonight, I wish I may, I wish I might, have the wish I wish tonight." Back then, I believed in the grandiosity of life.

After my sister died, so many of my hopes and dreams felt shattered and impossible. I simply didn't have the will or desire to create new ones. Having goals meant I had nothing to plan or work towards. I feel this was one of the biggest so-called mistakes I made for many years and one of the main reasons why I struggled for so long.

I gave up all of my hopes and dreams. I stopped wishing when I blew out birthday candles, and I certainly stopped my "silly" star-gazing wishes. I decided to just let life take me where it wanted to. Sometimes this approach worked out well for me but other times I roamed aimlessly without direction or fulfilment.

I lived without any fire burning inside of me, so it's no coincidence that when I didn't have any goals to chase or sense of purpose in my life, I was withdrawn, depressed and lost.

My advice is to never stop dreaming. In fact, spend time getting clear on what you want in life. It's a significant step towards avoiding that empty feeling, where you don't want to get out of bed each day. Just don't attach your happiness to the attainment of your goal.

I've studied so much about personal development and wonderful strategies for moving towards success. If you're in the place I was, I believe having goals is one of the best antidotes to coming back from that lifeless way of living.

Having goals is all about having something to look forward to. Short-term, midterm, and long-term goals are all important.

Is it important to set a purpose?

You don't really *set* a purpose. Your purpose is something that comes to you from within. But it is important to have a purpose, because it will give you the drive and fire in your belly. I don't believe people are born with a purpose laid out, but rather it's something that arises out of life experiences.

What do all humans have in common?

In 2006 I volunteered at an orphanage in India with a friend of mine. It's something I'd always wanted to do. It had a medical facility catering to children who had families with leprosy and was also a medical centre that provided care for anyone in the local area. What struck me was that no matter what language, age or religious barriers were between us, the need for love and connection was universal.

The children ranged from four to about eighteen. There were few adults at the orphanage, so the older children looked after the younger ones, but they were still kids themselves. However there was a clear message being sent. It was, *Wipe those tears. You'll be all right. Now toughen up*. But the message was sent with love.

My friend and I thought we'd be rolling up our sleeves and doing manual work. However, this orphanage wasn't set up for volunteers. They were actually self sufficient, with everyone living off the land and all pitching in doing their part. Their English was quite broken, and we didn't know the Indian dialect, so we were left with little to do.

Initially, we were disappointed, so we just played with the kids. In hindsight, I understand this was perfect. There was a void. The people in charge loved the children, but there were too few adults, so they didn't receive any real one-on-one attention. They gravitated towards us like we were celebrities, wanting to hold our hand and walk with us or sit on the swing, the only piece of play equipment, as we pushed it.

Although we had to contend with a language barrier, there was nothing that self-created sign and body language didn't overcome, with lots of guessing and laughter in between. We were in fits of giggles trying to speak to one another. It's fortunate that the kids learnt basic English at school. They taught us nursery rhymes and wanted us to sing to them. Mostly they just wanted our attention.

We didn't build a portable classroom or dig a well, but we lovingly connected to these children, and I think for the short time we were there, we fulfilled the universal desire people instinctively crave, which is love and connection.

What's driven you over the years?

My quest for freedom from my emotional pain. It's driven me to find the method that would liberate me and make the biggest difference in my life. Once I found it, I knew I wanted to help others with what I'd learnt.

What are you passionate about?

I'm passionate about the power of the mind, as well as the mind-body connection. I love understanding why people behave as they do and how to change beliefs, behaviours and feelings. I've loved learning about the power of appreciation, self-worth and the works of Abraham Hicks.

Is there a belief you used to have that's no longer relevant to you?

Yes. After Tahnee died I believed I knew what was, and wasn't, important in life. I thought I was wise and all-knowing about what truly mattered. I believed love was the most important thing in the world, and money didn't matter.

In my early twenties I didn't care for money. At one point, I was offered $20,000 a month to be a massage client's personal massage therapist. At the time I had a summer job lined up on an island in Australia. My ultimate dream was to work on an island, so that, among several other reasons, is why I declined.

For all of the blessings I've experienced in my life and luxury I've been privileged to enjoy, I've also experienced great opposites. I've had no money, no job, and at my worst, a friend let me live in her granny flat. Money became one of my biggest challenges. From these experiences, I learned that money is important. It won't give you happiness, but it is attached to so many areas of your life that can enhance your happiness. After your needs are met you can live more comfortably, so it's easier to fulfil your bucket list, contribute to society and help others.

I would never say money isn't important anymore. I appreciate it now.

What decisions have you made that resulted in a huge difference in your life?

I made a clear decision after my sister died that I would live my life differently from the average person by having many varied experiences. It was a purposeful decision and wasn't about aspiring to climb the corporate ladder or chase a career path. All I wanted upon taking my final breath was to know I'd experienced a full life.

I spent a short time living in America with my brother and travelled to Tasmania with a group of people in order to sell cleaning products. I also worked and lived my way around Australia, enjoying some of the continent's finest five-star resort destinations. I worked on the mines in harsh and remote but beautiful places in Western Australia and North Queensland, as well as retail in Western Australia. I sold tours in Uluru, massaged in Tasmania and did beauty therapy in Queensland and in the Victorian snowfields, to name just a few.

I drove across the Nullarbor on my own. In fact, I drove through many parts of our beautiful countryside on my own and with friends. I've also travelled internationally. I've been injured, out of work and out of money. I've been stuck. I've been free.

I spent several years in a de-facto relationship, committed and staying in one place. Even when I look back on my love life and breakups, I'm at peace. It's all part of the colourful tapestry of my life. I loved and lost, and I loved and gained. In the end, I'll know I gave it a red-hot go by having all of the varied experiences I said I would. Like the Frank Sinatra song says, I did it my way.

Have you had any mentors?

When I was in my twenties, I was blessed to have met Annie. She was about ten years older than I was. She shared her many life experiences with me, and I felt devastated by what she'd been through. She'd had numerous tragedies and hardships in her life, some of which singularly would have sent many other people into therapy, including the death of her older sister, which obviously was an area we connected on.

After my struggles with my sister's death and broken heart over a "failed" relationship a few months earlier, Annie really took me under her wing. She was my employer, and I was fortunate to experience her views on life virtually five days a week. Annie is amazing. She introduced me to another way of looking at life and different spiritual teachings. She has compassion for struggling people. She forgives those who did her wrong, and she overcame hardships and hurts. She loves people, and she just keeps going. People gravitate to Annie. She has such love for others and gives so much of herself. She's an example of the type of person I wanted to be.

I was raised by loving parents who taught me to be a kind and loving person. After Tahnee died, with my exposure to religion I wanted to be a good person, so I'd go to heaven and see Tahnee again. Meeting Annie was a turning point in my life. I wanted to be like her. To overcome challenges with dignity. To care about people and help them. To try and understand why they act the way they do, rather than feel resentful and blame them for my hurts. I no longer wanted to be a "good" person, so I'd see Tahnee again one day. I wanted to be a *kind and loving* person just because it's nice to be nice.

I had Annie on a pedestal when I worked for her, but over the years I began to see her more human traits. I allowed myself to be her friend rather than someone who didn't have anything to offer her wise and more knowing self. She never made me feel this way, but it's what I told myself. Today, I still hold Annie in great esteem, but these days I just see her as a fabulous person I feel privileged to call a friend.

What's one of the best experiences of your life?

I've had many fabulous experiences and times in my life. Many of them would involve the company of friends and family, but there is one experience I often fondly recall. When I lived on Hayman Island in the Whitsundays, I was standing on the sand looking over the water, admiring the stunning views and nearby island, when these butterflies appeared from nowhere and flew past me. There were a few to begin with and then thousands of them. They came from over the water and flew towards me, then straight past me. I was directly in their flight path and was surrounded by them. I was in awe of their majestic beauty and felt intertwined with nature in this perfect moment in time.

What services do you offer, and how can you help people?

I'm a life coach who specialises in emotions and mindset, and I use various modalities and powerful tools to achieve results. I expect my clients to take an active role in their transformation. In other words, I don't do the healing. I present different concepts and tools and lead my clients into action to facilitate change. I've done the work on myself and can only act as the beacon of light to let them know they, too, can transform and find peace. My clients do their part, I do my part, and together we collaborate. I walk with them as they grow and expand.

My coaching style is one of nurturing and encouragement. Although mindset is most important to me, I also value the power of physical and/or vibrational work, and may include them as a holistic, whole body and mind approach.

I've also started writing a book about my grief experiences. It starts when I was in the depths of my grief and goes all the way to twenty years later with my broader perspective. Whether I share it with the world or just with clients and others who may be going through the same experience remains to be seen, but I do feel it's time to share my story.

 To discover more about how Rebecca can help you *Elevate Your Life*, simply visit

www.elevate-books.com/life

Afterword

While you were reading these people's inspiring stories, did you notice something? All of their life experiences were for a purpose, bringing them closer to their goals, relationships and especially the message they were meant to share with the world.

The last page is a blank canvas for you to write the next chapter of your own story about elevating your life and inspiring others. Every day is a brand-new opportunity to be the author of your destiny.

Next Steps

To support you on your journey to *Elevate Your Life*, we recommend you take advantage of these resources:

7 Day Transformation Program

Learn ONE powerful 'Elevate Process' you can use immediately to improve Your Relationships, Health, Finances, Mindset and any other area of your life.

To join this 7-day transformation online program, simply go to: www.elevate-books.com/you

Connect with the Authors

To discover more about the authors and what they have to teach you, and bonus gifts they are offering visit:
www.elevate-books.com/life

Subscribe to our Podcast

If you'd like to hear the go-to interviews from the authors and be re-inspired, check out: www.elevate-books.com/podcast

Visit the Website

To find out more about the Elevate book series, visit: www.elevate-books.com

www.ingramcontent.com/pod-product-compliance
Lightning Source LLC
Chambersburg PA
CBHW071435080526
44587CB00014B/1862